PIONEERS OF SPACEFLIGHT

WRITTEN BY
MICHAEL O'NEILL

Danann
BOOKS

BOOKS

© Danann Publishing Ltd

First Published Danann Publishing Ltd 2018

CAT NO: DAN0422

Photography courtesy of NASA

Images courtesy of Getty Images:
Fine Art Images/Heritage Images; ITAR-TASS

All other; Wiki Commons

Layout & design Darren Grice at **Ctrl-d**

Made in EU.

ISBN: 978-1-912332-27-4

CONTENTS

INTRODUCTION

The vastness of the space beyond our own planet Earth fascinated mankind long before the first observation of the night sky through the telescope of the Italian Galileo Galilei in 1610. Its mysteries have not only fired the imaginations of scientists but also of novelists such as the Frenchman, satirist Cyrano De Bergerac, who wrote his fictional account of a journey to the moon in 1656, Histoire comique des états et empires de la lune, and in 1662 his account of a trip to the sun, Histoire comique des états et empires du soleil was published. Another Frenchman, Jules Verne, and the English historian and novelist H.G.Wells followed two centuries later. They entertained their readers with tales of outer space and of space travel that were based on scientific principles in line with the knowledge available at the time.

Interest in the vastness around us surged in the 20th century and spawned a myriad of science-fiction stories, and adventures with alien beings, on radio, film and TV, giving us such wondrous creatures as E.T. or Robin Williams as Mork in Mork and Mindy.

But since Yuri Gagarin completed the first orbit of the Earth in 1961, the last frontier has proven to be anything but a cosy backyard for mankind and has claimed the lives of many adventurous men and women who dared to undertake the journey into its vast darkness.

Space exploration has also yielded extraordinary scientific information that increases man's understanding of space, distant planets and galaxies and even the very first moments of our own universe. It has provided us with a greater understanding about our own planet and its solar systems and has even fostered greater cooperation between countries on Earth as they combine their scientific talents and knowledge in projects such as the International Space Station, in which the European Space Agency, the USA, Russia and Japan have all joined forces to produce benefits for many other nations such as South Africa and Nigeria, and proving, for example, that space technology can play an integral role in our understanding of Earth's ecology, helping to monitor climate change or the formulation of disaster management strategies.

Tangential to the activities in space, the technology required for cosmic exploration has led to advancements in many other fields such as public safety, health and medicine, information technology and weather satellites. Global search and rescue systems, solar panels, water purification and information on diet and food have also benefited from mankind's yearning to go far beyond the horizons of Earth.

The achievements to date have been impressive; singling out one achievement, Voyager 1, launched in 1977, is now about 13,000,000,000 miles from Earth. That is some 19.5 light hours away — although to put that into perspective, the nearest star is 4.24 light years away.

But even though humans are, as yet, only taking baby steps into space, limited by technical knowledge and expertise, there is no doubt that the exploration of space will continue to bring us astonishing discoveries and knowledge, and, perhaps, new homelands; hopefully before our sun collapses — in about 7.6 billion years from now.

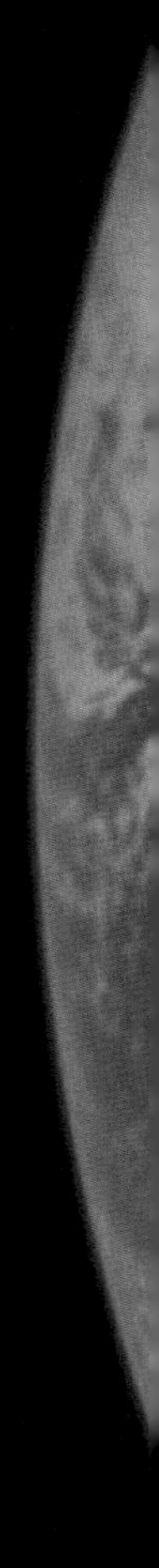

FAMOUS
ASTRONAUTS

SOVIET UNION YURI GAGARIN

Yuri Gagarin was born on March the 9th 1934 in the village of Klushino in the Smolensk Oblast in Russia. Drafted into the Soviet Air Force in 1955, Gagarin trained in jet fighters, and in 1960 he was selected to join the newly created Soviet Space Program.

As there was little room inside a spacecraft at that time, Gagarin, who was 5' 2" tall, was selected to join an elite band of cosmonauts known as the Sochi Six. These men formed the kernel of the Vostok space program.

"*Poyekhali!!*" With that one Russian word, meaning "*Let's go!*" on April the 12th 1961, cosmonaut Yuri Gagarin blasted off from the Baikonur Cosmodrome in Kazakhstan in Vostok 1 to become the first human to travel in space. His one-orbit flight lasted 108 minutes.

Upon his return from his historic single orbit of Earth, the Soviet Union treated Gagarin as a national hero. Completing many goodwill tours, he also became an international celebrity.

For several years, Soviet officials were hesitant to assign him to a second space flight for fear of losing him in an accident. He became deputy training director of the cosmonaut training centre, helping other cosmonauts prepare for their space flights and successfully completed his aerospace engineering thesis on space plane design at the prestigious Zhukovski Air Force Academy. Gagarin persisted in his desire to return to space, however, and he was eventually assigned as Vladimir Komarov's backup for the first Soyuz mission. After Komarov's death in the Soyuz 1 accident in April 1967, Soviet officials felt justified in their caution and Gagarin was never again allowed to train for or participate in further spaceflights.

RIGHT: Yuri Gagarin. A still from film 'The first flight to the stars'

BELOW LEFT: Yuri Gagarin with Academician S. Korolyov

BELOW RIGHT: Yuri Gagarin and Zakaria Mohieddin (the first on the right), Cairo Almaza Air Base, Egypt, 1962

On March the 27th 1968, while on a routine training mission from Chkalovskiy Air Base near the Star City cosmonaut training centre with flight instructor Vladimir Seryogin, the MiG-15UTI jet in which Gagarin was flying crashed in inclement weather, killing both pilots. Gagarin was 34. His ashes were interred in the Kremlin wall and are ritually visited by space flight crews prior to their departure for Baikonur.

Upon hearing the news, the NASA Astronaut Office sent a message of condolences to the Academy of Sciences of the U.S.S.R., saying in part: "*We join you in mourning the loss of Yuri Gagarin. Nothing will dim the memory of his achievement in becoming the first pilot to fly in space.*"

After his death, many prominent space facilities were renamed in his honour.

Outside Moscow, the facility where cosmonauts train for their spaceflights was renamed the Gagarin Cosmonaut Training Centre. Once a secret facility, today international crews, including U.S. astronauts, train there for missions to the international space station (ISS). At the Baikonur Cosmodrome, the launch pad from which Gagarin began his historic journey is known as the Gagarin Start. The pad is still in use today to launch multinational crews to the ISS.

To symbolise the current cooperation in space between two former rivals, in 2012 the Dialogue of Cultures — United World Foundation donated a bronze statue of Gagarin to the city of Houston, along with a bronze monument to John Glenn, the first American to orbit the Earth. The sculptures beside one another outside the building that was once the original headquarters of the Manned Spacecraft Centre (now the Lyndon B. Johnson Space Centre).

OPP. PAGE: Yuri Gagarin in capsule

ABOVE: USSR pilot-cosmonauts at a TV studio (from left to right): Pavel Popovich, Yuri Gagarin, Valentina Tereshkova, Valeri Bykovsky, Andrian Nikolayev and German Titov

LEFT: Yuri Gagarin in Warsaw,1961

USA
ALAN B SHEPARD JR

Alan Bartlett Shepard Jr. was born on the 18th of November 1923 in East Derry, NH. He graduated from the United States Naval Academy at Annapolis with a Bachelor of Science degree, and upon graduation married Louise Brewer, whom he met while at Annapolis. Shepard saw action in the US Navy during the second world war. In 1946, he became a naval aviator serving several tours aboard aircraft carriers and in 1950 attended Naval Test Pilot School at Patuxent River, MDS., where he became a test pilot and instructor. Graduating from the Naval War College at Newport, RI, Shepard was assigned to the staff of the commander-in-chief, Atlantic Fleet, as an aircraft readiness officer.

In 1959, Alan Shepard was selected to be an astronaut in NASA's Mercury Seven program. It was on May the 5th 1961, with a Redstone rocket that he made a 15-minute suborbital flight that took him and his Freedom 7 Mercury capsule to an altitude of 115 miles covering 302 miles downrange from Cape Canaveral, FL.
His flight came three weeks after the launch of the Soviet Vostok 1 carrying cosmonaut Yuri Gagarin on April the 12th 1961.

The flight of Freedom 7 was brief and did not achieve orbit; it was, nevertheless, a major step forward for the U.S. in a rapidly-accelerating race with the Soviet Union for dominance in the new arena of space.

Buoyed by the overwhelming response to Shepard's flight, which made the astronaut an instant hero and a household name, President John F. Kennedy set the nation on a course to a landing on the moon, declaring before a joint session of Congress just three weeks later, "*I believe this nation should commit itself to achieving the goal, before the decade is out, of landing a man on the moon and returning him safely to the Earth.*"

RIGHT: Astronaut Alan B. Shepard Jr., posing here in his Mercury flight suit, 1961

BELOW L_R: Astronaut Alan B. Shepard Jr., peers into his Freedom 7 Mercury capsule before launch on the morning of May 5, 1961 | Alan B. Shepard, Jr. sits in his Freedom 7 Mercury capsule, ready for launch | Alan Shepard is hurled into space atop a Mercury-Redstone rocket.

Over a three-and-a-half year period from July 1969 to December 1972, a dozen Americans explored the lunar surface.

Shepard, however, was almost bypassed for a trip to the moon. He had to overcome an inner ear problem called Meuniere's syndrome, which grounded him for several years following his initial pioneering flight.

An operation eventually cured the problem, and Shepard was selected to command the Apollo 14 mission. On January the 31st, 1971, Shepard, Command Module pilot Stuart Roosa and Lunar Module pilot Edgar Mitchell embarked for the Moon atop a Saturn 5 rocket. Shepard and Mitchell landed the lunar module Antares on February the 5th in the Fra Mauro Highlands on the near side of the moon while Roosa orbited overhead in the command ship Kitty Hawk.

Shepard planted his feet on the lunar surface a few hours later, declaring, "*Al is on the surface, and it's been a long way, but we're here.*" He was the fifth man to walk on the moon, and the oldest, at the age of 47.

During two excursions on the surface totalling nine hours, Shepard and Mitchell set up a science station, collected 92 pounds of rocks and gathered soil samples from the mountainous region. He was photographed playing golf, striking two balls across the lunar surface. Near the end of the second moonwalk, and just before entering the lunar module for the last time, Shepard (an avid golfer) hit two golf balls with a makeshift club. The first landed in a nearby crater. The second was hit squarely, and in the one-sixth gravity of the moon, Shepard reported that it travelled "*miles and miles and miles.*"

In August 1974, Shepard, by then a rear admiral, retired from both NASA and the Navy and became chairman of Marathon Construction Corp. in Houston. He later founded his own business company, Seven Fourteen Enterprises, named after his two missions on Freedom 7 and Apollo 14.

Alan Shepard died of leukaemia on July the 21st 1998. His wife Louise died five weeks later. Their marriage had lasted for 53 years.

OPP. PAGE: Awaiting Mercury Redstone 3 launch, 1961

TOP: Edgar Mitchell, left, and Alan Shepard in lunar surface simulation training at the Kennedy Space Center, 1970

ABOVE: During training for the Apollo 14 mission stands in front of the Lunar Landing Research Vehicle

RIGHT: Apollo 14 launch vehicle lifts off from Pad 39A at the Kennedy Space Center, 1971

LEFT: Alan Shepard Completes His Mission, 1961

ABOVE LEFT: The Apollo 14 command module with astronauts Alan Shepard, Stuart A. Roosa and Edgar Mitchell aboard approaches touchdown in the South Pacific Ocean, 1971

ABOVE RIGHT: Alan B. Shepard Jr. walks away from his Freedom 7 capsule following a post-flight inspection aboard the carrier USS Champlain, 1961

SOVIET UNION
VALENTINA TERESHKOVA

Born on March the 6th 1937, in the Yaroslavl Oblast in central Russia, Tereshkova's father had been killed during the Second World War and after school she found employment as a textile worker in a local factory. Interested in parachuting from a young age, it was during this time that she became an experienced parachutist. She also became a member of the local Young Communist League, and later joined the Communist Party of the Soviet Union. Her parachuting expertise and party affiliation helped win her selection to, and made her a leading candidate in, the woman cosmonaut program. Major General Nikolai Kamanin, the official in charge of cosmonaut training, felt that Tereshkova should fly first, noting in his diary that "*she is active in society, is especially pleasing in appearance, makes use of her great authority among everyone who she knows.... We must first send Tereshkova into space.*"

Alongside Tereshkova's expertise in parachuting, the fact that her father was a war hero from the Russo-Finnish War was another essential element that led to her being selected; pilots in Vostok would have to parachute from the capsule following re-entry. And she was a proletarian.

On the morning of June the 16th 1963, Vostok 6 blasted off on a mission of 48 orbits around the Earth carrying Valentina Tereshkova, the first woman to go into space. While orbiting the Earth for almost three days, Valentina Tereshkova conducted a number of experiments, took photographs and recorded flight notes.

Following her historic flight, she landed safely having parachuted down on re-entry.

Although she would never fly again, her role in the historic flight and her moving life story and accomplishments were held up as an example for others to follow. Her voyage inspired women around the world to reach for their dreams and set their sights on the stars.

Following her flight, Tereshkova was swept into Soviet politics, serving

RIGHT: Valentina Tereshkova, 1969

BELOW L-R: Valentina Tereshova, 1964 | Valentina Tereshkova prepares for mission | Vostok-6 descent module

as a member of the Supreme Soviet, the Presidium of the Supreme Soviet and the Central Committee of the Communist Party. She also became a well-known representative of the Soviet Union abroad, acting as the Soviet representative to the UN Conference for International Women's Year in 1975 and leading the Soviet delegation to the World Conference on Women in Copenhagen. She was awarded the Joliot-Curie Gold Medal of Peace for her work with the World Peace Council.

With the exception of the single flight by Tereshkova, human spaceflight during the early years of the space race was the province of men only. Women demonstrated their ability to withstand the rigours of space missions, and indeed a hardy group of American women pilots passed the same medical tests as the Mercury Seven with excellent scores. However, NASA policy at the time required qualification as a military test pilot. The policy, originally established by President Eisenhower in December 1958, stood until the mid-1960s when the first scientist-astronauts were selected. Although the Eisenhower selection policy did not specifically discriminate on the basis of gender, the fact that there were no women military pilots (never mind test pilots) made it clear that women would not become U.S. astronauts at that time. For its part, by sending a woman into space the Soviet Union had put the U.S on the back foot and proven U.S. policy to be wrong.

In April 1962, five women were chosen for the Soviet program. Among them only the 25-year-old Valentina Tereshkova ever flew in space. Nineteen years later, after the U.S. had recruited women into the astronaut corps the Soviet Union trained Svetlana Savitskaya and launched her on a mission to the Salyut 7 space station in the summer of 1982; thus making sure that the first two women in space were Soviet citizens. (Savitskaya flew a second time in 1984 and became the first woman to do a space walk.)

CCCP

OPP. PAGE LEFT: Valentina Tereshkova, on the day when she piloted Vostok 6, making the first space flight by a woman, 16 June 1963

OPP. PAGE RIGHT: Vostok 6 launch

ABOVE LEFT: Walter Ulbricht Stadium, Hungary

ABOVE RIGHT: Looking over the Apollo Command Module on exhibit in Building 2 during a tour of the Johnson Space Center in 1977 with astronaut Alan Bean

USA
SALLY RIDE

Sally Kristen Ride was born in Los Angeles on the 26th of May 1951. She attended Portola Junior High then Birmingham High School and was awarded a scholarship to study at the Westlake School for Girls, a private school in Los Angeles. She then attended Swathmore College, and at the University of California she took physics courses. She graduated from Stanford University with a bachelor's degree in English and Physics, then studied at Stanford for a master's degree and a PhD in physics having carried out research in astrophysics and free electron laser physics. It was while she was at Stanford that she answered an advertisement in the student newspaper asking for applicants to join the NASA space program. She sent in an application, along with 8,000 other people, and was one of only 35 chosen to join the astronaut corps. Joining NASA in 1978, she served as the ground-based capsule communicator, or capcom, for the second and third space shuttle missions (STS-2 and STS-3) and helped with development of the space shuttle's robotic arm.

One of six women selected in NASA's 1978 astronaut class, Sally Ride was the first of them to fly. When she rode aboard the space shuttle Challenger as it lifted off from Kennedy Space Center on June the 18th 1983, she became the first American woman in space, capturing the nation's attention and imagination as another symbol of the ability of women to break barriers. As one of the three mission specialists on the STS-7 mission, she played a vital role in helping the crew deploy communications satellites, conduct experiments and make use of the first Shuttle Pallet Satellite. Her voyage and interesting life helped, as President Barack Obama said, to "*inspire generations of young girls to reach for the stars*", for she "*showed us that there are no limits to what we can achieve.*"

After her selection for the crew of STS-7, and thereby becoming the first American woman in space, Ride faced intense media attention. But, she had no time for many of the questions the press asked her; questions like

BELOW LEFT: Shuttle mission simulator training for Challenger's second space mission

BELOW RIGHT: Astronaut Robert L. Crippen (center, first row) is crew commander. Other crew members are astronauts Frederick H. Hauck, right, pilot; and Sally K. Ride, John M. Fabian and Norman E. Thagard, mission specialists

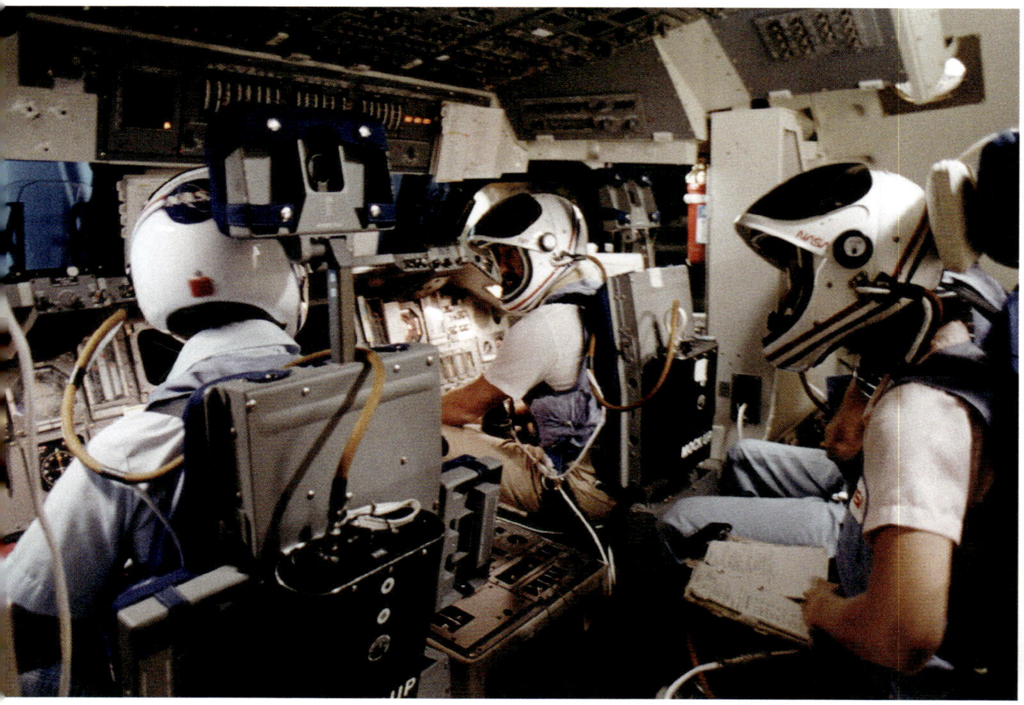

"*Do you weep when things go wrong on the job?*" She saw herself first and foremost as an astronaut and a scientist, and felt that "*one thing I probably share with everyone else in the astronaut office is composure.*" Talking about her fellow astronauts in the class of 1978, she said, "*We're all people who are dedicated to the space program and who really want to fly in the space shuttle. That's a common characteristic that we all have that transcends the different backgrounds.*" (That astronaut class of 1978 also included the first three African-Americans and the first Asian-American to serve in the astronaut corps.) Ride's commander on STS-7, Bob Crippen, agreed that Sally extremely capable, saying, "*I wanted a competent engineer who was cool under stress. Sally had demonstrated that talent.*"

Ride continued her career with NASA after her historic flight, flying on a second shuttle mission (STS-41G) in October 1984. Later, she served on the presidential commission that investigated the Challenger accident and also led NASA's strategic planning effort in the mid-1980s.

Retiring from NASA in 1987, she became a science fellow at the Center for International Security and Arms Control at Stanford University and, in 1989, joined the University of California-San Diego as a professor of physics and director of the California Space Institute. In 2001, she founded her own company, Sally Ride Science, to pursue her passion for motivating girls and boys to study the STEM fields-science, technology, engineering and math.

In addition to this work, she wrote a number of science books for children, including The Third Planet, which won the American Institute of Physics Children's Science Writing Award in 1995. Following a 17-month long battle with pancreatic cancer, Sally Ride died on June 23, 2012, leaving behind a heroic legacy.

Valentina Tereshkova and Sally Ride, as the first women from their respective countries to fly in space, helped to usher in an era of equality in human spaceflight, paving the way for more than 55 more women to also journey into space.

Sally Ride continued to help students, girls in particular, study science and mathematics, until her death on July the 23rd 2012.

OPP PAGE LEFT: The seven member crew leaves the Operations and Checkout Building (OCB) while on their way to the launch pad

OPP PAGE RIGHT: The seventh launch of the NASA Space Transportation System and the second for Challenger

ABOVE LEFT & RIGHT: Sally Ride, STS-7 mission specialist on the flight deck of the Earth-orbiting Space Shuttle Challenger

USA
JOHN GLENN JR

John Herschel Glenn Jr. saw the light of day on July the 18th 1921 in Cambridge, Ohio. His primary and secondary schools were in New Concord, Ohio, and he was a student in Muskingum College in New Concord, where he gained a bachelor of science degree in engineering. His former college was one of nine colleges or universities that later awarded him honorary doctoral degrees.

Glenn entered the Naval Aviation Cadet Program in March 1942. He graduated and was commissioned in the Marine Corps in 1943. After advanced training, he joined Marine Fighter Squadron 155 and spent a year flying F-4U fighters in the Marshall Islands. He flew 59 combat missions during World War II.

After the war, he was a member of Marine Fighter Squadron 218 on the North China patrol and served on Guam. From June 1948 to December 1950 he served as an instructor in advanced flight training at Corpus Christi, Texas. He then attended Amphibious Warfare Training at Quantico, VA.

In the Korean war, he flew 63 missions with Marine Fighter Squadron 311. As an exchange pilot with the Air Force, Glenn flew 27 missions in the F-86 Sabre. In the last nine days of fighting in Korea, Glenn shot down three MiGs in combat along the Yalu River.

From November 1956 to April 1959, Glenn worked for the Fighter Design Branch of the Navy Bureau of Aeronautics (now the Bureau of Naval Weapons) in Washington. Whilst he was there, he also studied at the University of Maryland.

He was a project officer of the F-8U Crusader, when in July 1957, he set a transcontinental speed record during the first transcontinental flight to average supersonic speed. Flying from Los Angeles to New York, he covered the distance in 3 hours and 23 minutes.

BELOW L-R: 1962, Project Mercury Astronaut John H. Glenn Jr | John H. Glenn Jr.'s balance mechanism (semi-circular-canals) is tested by running cool water into his ear and measuring effect on eye motions | John H. Glenn Jr. (left), Dr. William Douglas, astronauts flight surgeon, and equipment specialist Joe Schmitt leave crew quarters prior to Mercury-Atlas 6 (MA-6) mission. Glenn is in his pressure suit and is carrying the portable ventilation unit

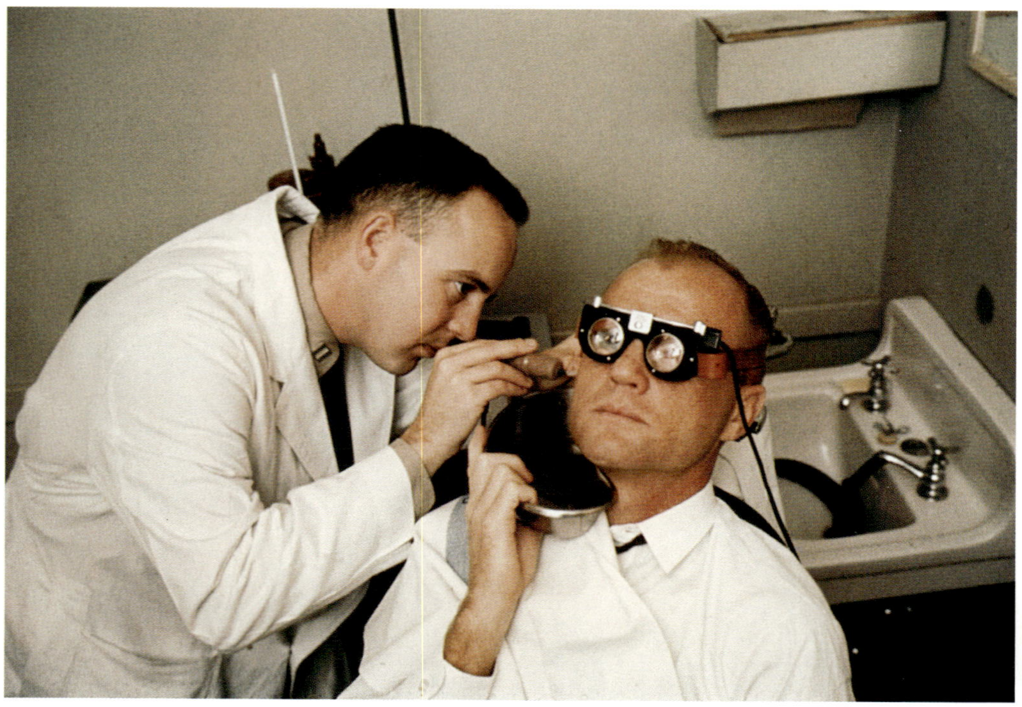

From 1974 Glenn served four terms as a U.S. senator from Ohio in a political career that took him to December 1998 when he retired.

Glenn was one of NASA's original Mercury Seven astronauts, test pilots selected by NASA in 1959 as the United States' first astronauts and was then chosen to be America's first man in space. After 70 simulated missions and training his reactions to 189 simulated system failures, he began his flight on Friendship 7 on February the 20th 1962.

The automatic-control system failed during Glenn's first orbit, which forced him to operate in manual mode during orbits two and three and for re-entry. Later, telemetry indicated that the heat shield had come loose. Large pieces of flaming debris flew past his capsule window during re-entry, which, fortunately, belonged to the rocket pack and not the heat shield. "*It made for a very spectacular re-entry from where I was sitting*", he joked later.

His mission of almost nine days on the space shuttle orbiter Discovery, launched October the 29th 1998, when he was 77, made him the oldest human to venture into space. On Discovery, he participated in a series of tests on the ageing process. The ageing population was one focus of his work as a U.S. senator. The crew handled a variety of research payloads and deployed the Spartan solar-observing spacecraft, the Hubble Space Telescope Orbital Systems Test Platform.

Glenn was described as "*humble, funny, and generous*" by Trevor Brown, dean of the John Glenn School of Public Affairs at Ohio State University. "*Even after leaving public life, he loved to meet his fellow citizens, school children in particular. He thrilled to music and had a weakness for chocolate.*"

He was considered one of the Senate's leading experts on technical and scientific matters, and won wide respect for his work to prevent the spread of weapons of mass destruction. He took pride in using his position on the Governmental Affairs Committee to root out waste in government and to clean up the nation's nuclear materials production plants.

John Glenn died on Thursday December the 8th 2016 at the Ohio State University Wexner Medical Center in Columbus.

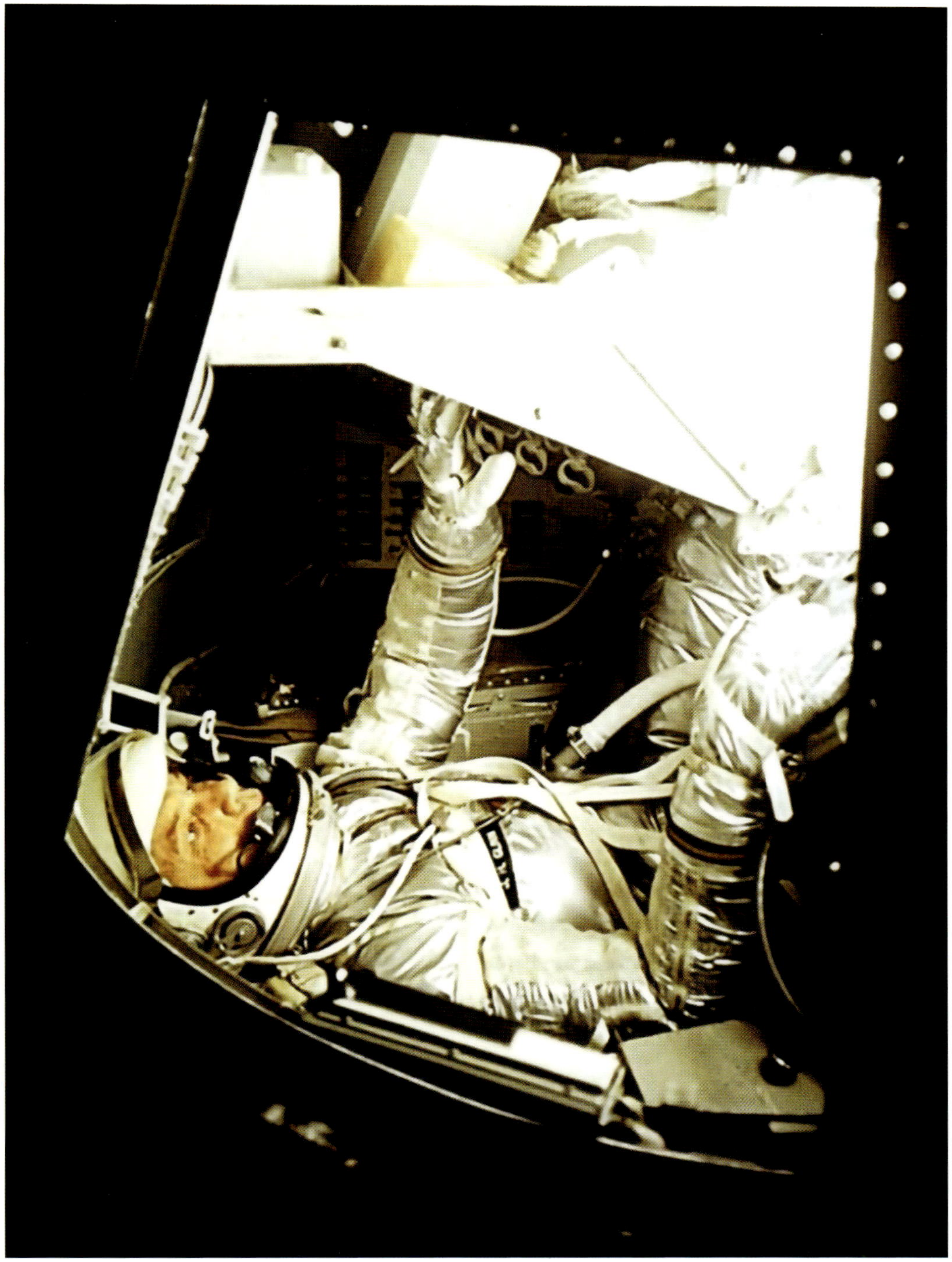

OPP. PAGE: The first group of astronauts announced by the NASA. They were selected in April of 1959 for the Mercury Program. Front row, L-R, Walter M. Schirra Jr., Donald K. Slayton, John H. Glenn Jr., and M. Scott Carpenter. Back row, L-R, are Alan B. Shepard Jr., Virgil I. Grissom and L. Gordon Cooper Jr

ABOVE LEFT: John H. Glenn Jr., wearing a Mercury pressure suit

ABOVE RIGHT: Training for MA-6 mission

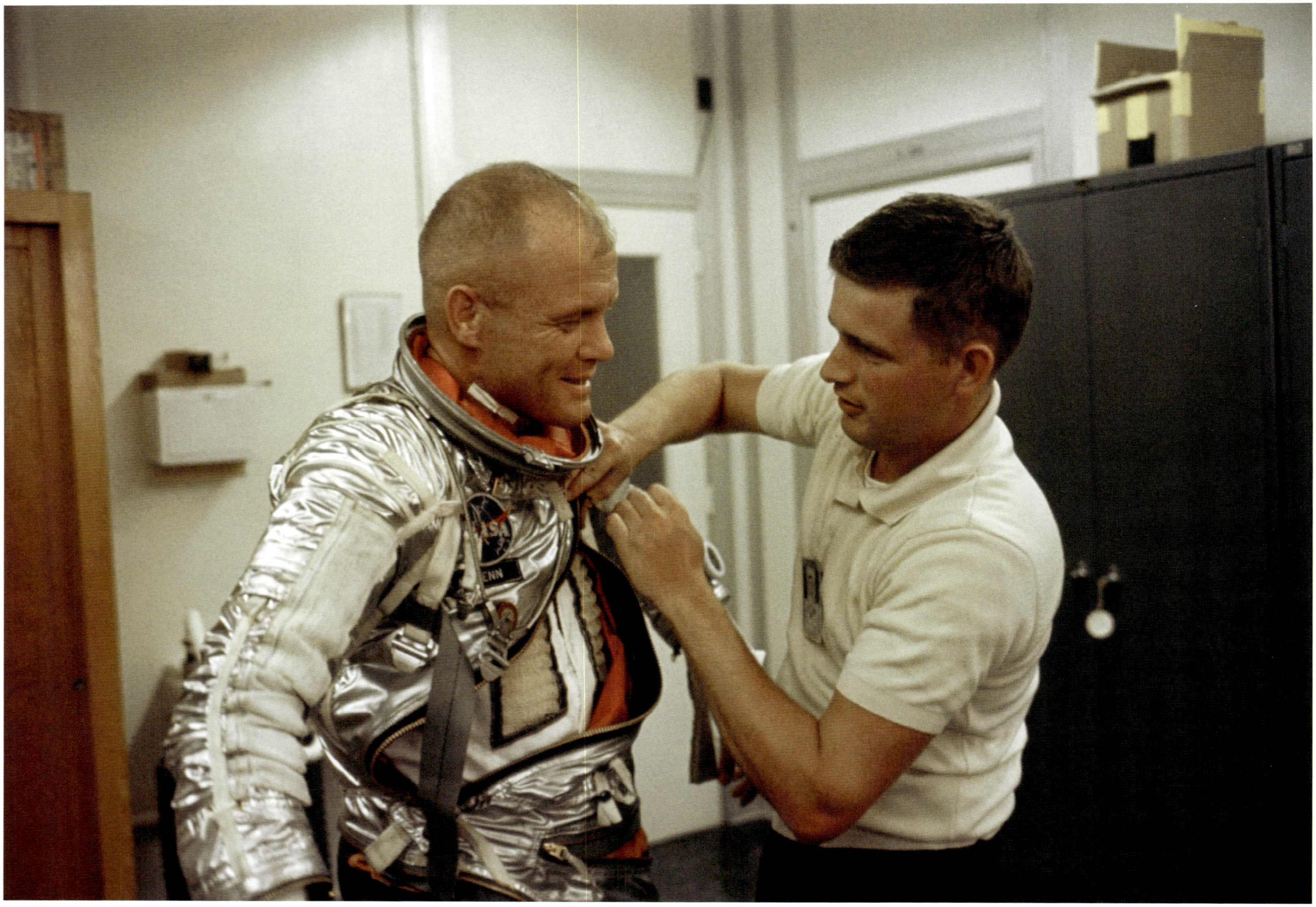

ABOVE: John H. Glenn Jr., pilot of the Mercury-Atlas 6 Earth-orbital space mission, is suited up at Cape Canaveral, Florida, during MA-6 preflight activities. Assisting Glenn is suit technician Al Rochford

OPP. PAGE LEFT: Mercury Atlas-6 lifts off on Feb. 20, 1962

OPP. PAGE RIGHT TOP & BELOW: A camera onboard the "Friendship 7" Mercury spacecraft photographs astronaut John H. Glenn Jr. during his Mercury-Atlas 6 spaceflight

USA
NEIL ARMSTRONG

Neil A. Armstrong, the first man to walk on the moon, was born on August the 5th 1930 in Wapakoneta. Armstrong signed up for three years of military service as a naval aviator before completing his degree at Purdue University. He trained on jet aircraft and became a test pilot, serving on the National Advisory Committee for Aeronautics for the High-Speed Flight Station prior to becoming an astronaut.

After serving as a naval aviator from 1949 to 1952, Armstrong joined the National Advisory Committee for Aeronautics (NACA) in 1955. His first assignment was with the NACA Lewis Research Center (now NASA Glenn) in Cleveland. Over the next 17 years, he was an engineer, test pilot, astronaut and administrator for NACA and its successor agency, the National Aeronautics and Space Administration (NASA).

As a research pilot at NASA's Flight Research Center, Edwards, Calif., he was a project pilot on many pioneering high speed aircraft, including the well known, 4000-mph X-15. He flew over 200 different models of aircraft, including jets, rockets, helicopters and gliders.

In 1962, after the Mercury Seven program, NASA wanted to create a second group of astronauts for the Gemini program. Armstrong transferred to astronaut status that same year. He was assigned as command pilot for the Gemini 8 mission, which was launched on March the 16th 1966, during which Armstrong performed the first successful docking of two vehicles in space.

Gemini 11 was launched that same year and Armstrong was backup pilot on that mission. With Apollo 8 still orbiting the moon, Armstrong was then offered commander spot on the Apollo 11 flight.

On July the 16th 1969, as spacecraft commander on the first

BELOW LEFT: Neil Armstrong, wearing an Extravehicular Mobility Unit, participates in a simulation of deploying and using lunar tools on the surface of the moon in Building 9, April 22, 1969

BELOW MIDDLE & RIGHT: Training exercise in Building 9, 1969. Edwin E. Aldrin Jr. (on left), lunar module pilot, uses a scoop to pick up a sample. Astronaut Neil Armstrong, Apollo 11 commander, holds bag to receive sample

manned lunar landing mission on Apollo 11 with his crew of Buzz Aldrin and Michael Collins, Armstrong gained the distinction of being the first man to land a craft, the lunar module, on the moon, and the first to step onto its surface.

As he did so he spoke the famous words, *"That's one small step for a man, one giant leap for mankind."*

Armstrong subsequently held the position of Deputy Associate Administrator for Aeronautics, NASA Headquarters, Washington, D.C. In this position, he was responsible for the coordination and management of overall NASA research and technology work related to aeronautics.

He was Professor of Aerospace Engineering at the University of Cincinnati between 1971-1979. During the years 1982-1992, Armstrong was chairman of Computing Technologies for Aviation, Inc., Charlottesville, VA.

He received a Bachelor of Science Degree in Aeronautical Engineering from Purdue University and a Master of Science in Aerospace Engineering from the University of Southern California. He holds honorary doctorates from a number of universities and also a number of fellowships. He was a member of the National Academy of Engineering and the Academy of the Kingdom of Morocco, serving as a member of the National Commission on Space (1985-1986), as Vice-Chairman of the Presidential Commission on the Space Shuttle Challenger Accident (1986), and as Chairman of the Presidential Advisory Committee for the Peace Corps (1971-1973).

Awarded decorations by 17 countries, the recipient of many special honours, Neil Armstrong passed away on August the 25th 2012 following complications resulting from cardiovascular procedures. He was 82. His remains were scattered in the Atlantic Ocean.

ABOVE: Neil Armstrong, 1963

RIGHT: Gemini-8 Astronauts Neil A. Armstrong, Command Pilot, and David R. Scott, Pilot, arrive at White Room, Complex 19 to enter Spacecraft for Simulation Test, 1966

FAR RIGHT: Recovery with Astronauts Neil A. Armstrong, Command Pilot and David R. Scott, Pilot in pacific after their GT-8 Flight, 1966

FAR LEFT: 363-feet tall Apollo 11 (Spacecraft 107/Lunar Module 5/Saturn 506) space vehicle is launched from Pad A, Launch Complex 39, Kennedy Space Center (KSC), at 9:32 a.m. (EDT), July 16, 1969

LEFT: Inside the Lunar Module (LM) while the LM rested on the lunar surface

ABOVE: The Apollo 11 crewmen, wearing biological isolation garments, arrive aboard the USS Hornet during recovery operations in the central Pacific. They are walking toward the Mobile Quarantine Facility (MQF), in which they will be confined until they arrive at the Manned Spacecraft Center's (MSC), Lunar Receiving Laboratory

USA
JAMES A LOVELL JR

Born on the 25th of March 1928, in Cleveland, Ohio, Lovell was interested in rocketry and built flying models from an early age. Graduating from the University of Wisconsin with a bachelor of science degree, and from the United States Naval Academy, he was selected as one of the Mercury Seven, serving as a pilot. In 1952; he attended Test Pilot School, NATC, Patuxent River, Maryland, and in 1958; the Aviation Safety School, University of Southern California. He followed this with the Advanced Management Program, Harvard Business School in 1971, being awarded several honorary doctorates.

Lovell spent 4 years as a test pilot at the Naval Air Test Center, Patuxent River, Maryland. Whilst he was there, he was Program Manager for the F4H "*Phantom*" Fighter and was a Safety Engineer with the Fighter Squadron 101 at the Naval Air Station, Oceana, Virginia.

Lovell married the former Marilyn Gerlach, of Milwaukee, Wisconsin and they had four children.

James Lovell was selected as an Astronaut by NASA in September 1962 and took the role of backup pilot for the Gemini 4 flight and backup Commander for the Gemini 9 flight. On the Apollo 11 lunar landing mission, he was backup Commander to Neil Armstrong.

It was December the 4th 1965 when he and Frank Borman were launched into space on the historic Gemini 7 mission. That flight lasted 330 hours and 35 minutes and saw the first rendezvous of two manned, manoeuvrable spacecraft with the Gemini-Agena Target Vehicle (GATV).

Lovell then took command on the Gemini 12 mission, with Pilot Edwin Aldrin on board, which started on the 11th of November 1966. This flight lasted for 4 days, making 59 revolutions and brought the Gemini program to a close.

BELOW L-R: James A. Lovell Jr. (left) and Fred W. Haise Jr., carry out a simulation of a lunar traverse at Kilauea, Hawaii | James A. Lovell Jr. (left) talks with NASA spacesuit technician Clyde Teague during suiting up procedures at Launch Complex 16, Kennedy Space Center. | Dr. Charles A. Berry checks astronaut James A. Lovell Jr., Gemini-7 prime crew pilot, following a workout on an exercise machine

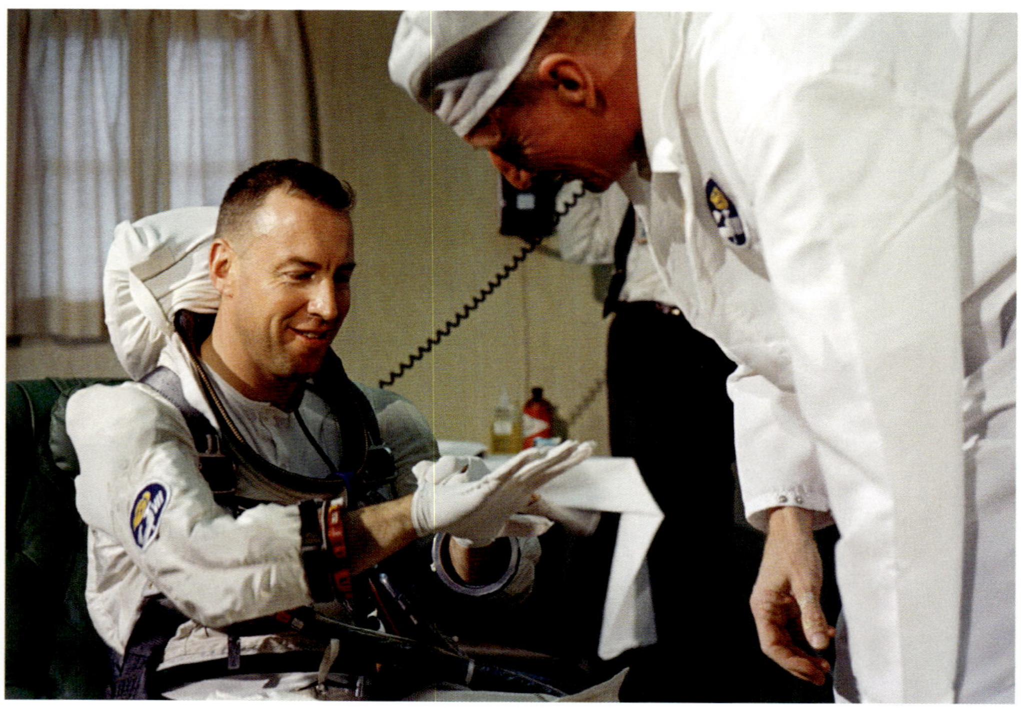

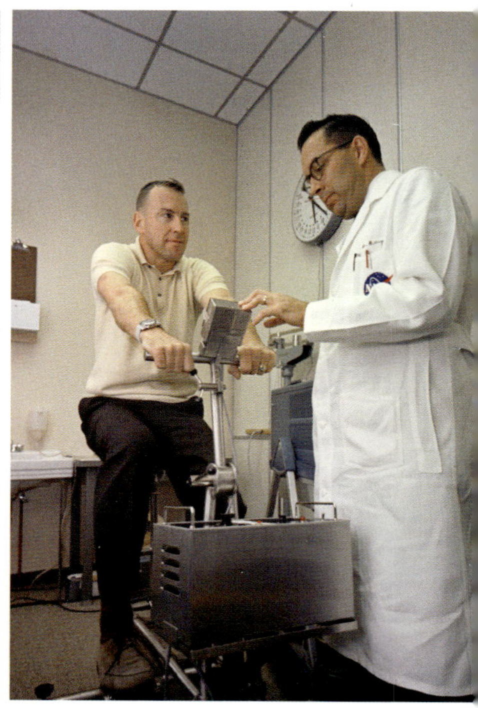

As Command Module pilot and navigator, Lovell was on board on for Apollo 8's six-day journey to the moon, the first craft to enter lunar orbit, which took place between the 21st and 27th of December 1968. Lovell and fellow crewmen Frank Borman and William A. Anders, became the first humans to leave the Earth's gravitational influence, having been pushed into near-Earth orbit by the seven-and-a-half-million-pound thrust of Apollo 8's Saturn V launch vehicle.

Lovell is most remembered for his role on his fourth mission as Spacecraft Commander of the Apollo 13 flight between the 11th and 17th of April 1970. Originally scheduled for ten days, Apollo 13's flight plan was modified en route to the moon due to a failure of the Service Module cryogenic oxygen system. (Cryogenics relates to the production of — and behaviours of materials at — very low temperatures.) A fire started inside an oxygen tank and liquid oxygen was converted into high pressure gas. This burst the tanks and led to a second oxygen tank springing a leak. It took just over two hours for all oxygen to be lost from the craft, thus rendering the hydrogen fuel cells for the Command Service Module to be disabled. These cells gave the module its electrical power. The lunar landing was aborted and the task became one of getting the men safely back down to Earth.

Lovell and fellow crewmen, John L. Swigert and Fred W. Haise, working closely with Houston ground controllers, converted their lunar module "*Aquarius*" into an effective lifeboat. Their emergency activation and operation of lunar module systems conserved enough electrical power and water to assure their safety and survival while in space and for the return to Earth. Swinging around the moon and adjusting the flight course twice, Lovell landed the craft safely on April the 17th.

Lovell became the first man to journey twice to the moon and only one of three in total. He was also the first man to fly into space four times.

With a total of 715 hours and 5 minutes in space, James Lovell held the record for time away from the Earth until surpassed by the Skylab flights.

Lovell retired from the Navy and from the Space Program on the 1st of March 1973.

ABOVE: Relaxing in the suiting up trailer at Launch Complex 16, during Gemini-7 prelaunch countdown at Cape Kennedy, Florida

RIGHT: Astronaut James A. Lovell Jr., is hoisted aboard a helicopter from the USS Iwo Jima, prime recovery vessel for the mission

OPP. PAGE: Prime crew of the Apollo 8 lunar orbit mission. Left to right, are James A. Lovell Jr., command module pilot; William A. Anders, lunar module pilot; and Frank Borman, commander. They are standing beside the Apollo Mission Simulator at the Kennedy Space Center

THE
END

LEFT: Gemini 12 crew arrives at Launch Complex 19. Lovell is followed by Edwin E. "Buzz" Aldrin Jr. The signs on their backs note that this mission is the final flight of the Gemini Program

ABOVE LEFT: Safe splashdown of the Apollo 13 Command Module (CM) in the South Pacific

ABOVE RIGHT: Crew men aboard the USS Iwo Jima, prime recovery ship for the Apollo 13 mission, hoist the Command Module (CM) aboard ship

A BRIEF TIMELINE OF SPACE EXPLORATION

1944

Germany launches first spaceflight in history, a V-2 rocket.

1946 – 10TH MAY

America sends first space research flight into space on an improved V-2 rocket.

1946 – 22ND MAY

First US rocket reaches the edge of space; 49 miles.

1946 – 24TH OCTOBER

America receives first pictures of the Earth from height of 65 miles.

1947 - 20TH FEBRUARY

America sends fruit flies into space as the first living creatures.

1951 - 2ND JULY

Russians send first dogs into space.

1957 - 26TH AUGUST

Russia fires the first intercontinental ballistic missile.

1957 – 4TH OCTOBER.

Russia sends the first artificial satellite into space and receives the first signals from space from Sputnik 1.

1957 – 3RD NOVEMBER

Russia sends the first animal into space orbit in Sputnick 2, the dog Laika.

1958 - 31ST JANUARY

The USA sends Explorer 1 into space to confirm the existence of the Van Allen radiation belts.

1959 – 2ND JANUARY

Russia executes the first firing of a rocket orbiting the Earth; first detection of solar winds; the propulsive manoeuvre known as trans-lunar injection is used (TLI sets a spacecraft on a trajectory towards the moon).

1959 – 4TH JANUARY

Russia sends first artificial satellite to the vicinity of the moon; the first artificial satellite to enter a heliocentric orbit.

1959 – 7TH AUGUST

America receives the first photograph of Earth from orbit.

1959 – 13TH SEPTEMBER

Russia sends the Luna 2 spacecraft on to the moon; it was the first spacecraft to reach the Lunar surface and the first man-made object to touch down on another celestial body.

1959 – 4TH OCTOBER

Russia received the first photographs of another planet from space from Luna 3, which photographs the far side of the moon.

1960 - 11TH MARCH

America sends the first solar probe into space, Pioneer 5.

1960 – 19TH AUGUST

Russia brings back the first plants and animals alive on Sputnik 5.

1960 – 10TH OCTOBER

Russia sends the first probe towards Mars, Mars 1M, which fails to reach its destination.

1961 – 31ST JANUARY

America sends the first primate into space, the chimpanzee Ham, who performs the first tasks in a spacecraft.

1961 – 12TH FEBRUARY

Russia achieves first launch of an upper stage from an Earth orbit into a heliocentric orbit and carries out the first spin stabilisation and midcourse corrections.

1961 – 12TH OF APRIL

The Russian astronaut Yuri Gagarin is the first man in space aboard Vostok 1. This was also the first manned orbital flight.

1961 – 5TH MAY

The USA achieves the first flight by a spacecraft piloted by a human, Alan Shepard, the first suborbital flight crewed by a human and the first landing with the pilot still in the spacecraft, Mercury-Redstone 3 or Freedom 7.

1961 – 19TH OF MAY

The Russians are the first to achieve a planetary flyby of Venus when Venera 1 passed within 100,000 km of the planet.

1962 – 7TH MARCH

America launches OSO1, the first Solar observatory to go into orbit.

1962 – 26TH OF APRIL

America sends the Ranger 4; Impact on the far side of the moon for the first time.

1962 – NOVEMBER

Russia sends Mars 1 to within 11,000 km of Mars.

1962 – 14TH DECEMBER

America sends Mariner 2 to within 34,773 km of Venus.

1963 – 16TH JUNE

Russia sends Valentina Tereshkova as the first woman into space on Vostok 6.

1963 – 19TH OF JULY

America launches a reusable manned spacecraft; X-15 Flight 90.

1965 – 14TH JULY

America sends Mariner 4 to within 9,846 kilometres of Mars. Close-up photographs of the surface are received on Earth.

1966 – 3RD FEBRUARY

Russia lands Luna 9 on the moon achieving the first softer landing on another celestial body.

1966 – 16TH MARCH

America docks to spacecraft for the first time; Gemini 8 and in the Agena Target Vehicle.

1966 – 3RD APRIL

Russia sends Luna 10 around the moon, the first artificial satellite to do so.

1967 – 30TH OCTOBER

Russia carries out the first automated docking, which takes place between Cosmos 186 and Cosmos 188. Soyuz 1 crashes.

1968 - 22ND SEPTEMBER

On Zond 5, Russia brings back safely to Earth the first plants and animals to orbit the moon.

1969 – 16TH JANUARY

Russia achieves the first crew exchange in space after successfully docking to manned spacecraft in an Earth orbit; Soyuz 4 and Soyuz 5.#

1969 – 16TH MAY

Russia parachutes Venera 5 into Venus's atmosphere.

1969 – 20TH JULY

America lands the first human on the moon in Apollo 11 and achieves the first space launch from another celestial body.

1969 – 19TH NOVEMBER

Apollo 12 and Surveyor 3 achieve the first double landing on a celestial body.

1970 – 24TH SEPTEMBER

Russia sends the first lunar rover to the moon with Lunokhod 1.

1970 – 15TH DECEMBER

Russia launches Venera 7 which achieves the first soft landing on Venus.

1971 – 19TH APRIL

Russia launches the first space station, Salyut 1.

1971 – 2ND DECEMBER

Russia sends Mars 3 to make the first soft landing on Mars and send back the first signals.

1972 – 15TH JULY

America sends Pioneer 10 into the asteroid belt and it leaves the inner solar system.

1975 – 15TH JULY

Russia and America create the first multinational manned mission with Apollo and Soyuz spacecraft.

1976 – 17TH APRIL

The Americans send Helios 2 to within 43,432,000 kilometres of the sun.

1979 – 1ST SEPTEMBER

Pioneer 11 makes the first flyby of Saturn at a distance of 21,000 km, sending photographs of Titan to Earth.

1981 – 12TH APRIL

STS-1 is the first reusable manned spacecraft from the USA.

1983 – 13TH JUNE

The American Pioneer 10 is the first spacecraft to pass beyond all solar system planets.

1986 – 28TH JANUARY

The crew of the American Challenger spacecraft is lost in space following an explosion.

1992 – 8TH FEBRUARY

First polar orbit around the Sun by NASA and ESA.

1995 – 22ND MARCH

The Russian spacecraft Mir achieves the longest spaceflight staying in space for 437.7 days with astronaut Valeri Polyakov.

1997 – 4TH JULY

The American Mars Pathfinder on Mars is the first operational rover on another planet.

1998 – 20TH NOVEMBER

The international space station, a cooperation between Russia, the USA, Europe, Japan, and Canada, becomes the largest man-made object built in space.

2001 – 12TH FEBRUARY

NASA makes the first landing on an asteroid with NEAR Shoemaker on 433 Eros.

2005 – 14TH JANUARY

Cassini-Huygens, a co-operation between Europe, America and Italy, achieves the first soft landing on Titan.

2009 – 6TH MARCH

America launches the Kepler Mission, a space telescope created specifically to search for Earth-like exoplanets.

2014 – 12TH NOVEMBER

The European Space Agency (ESA) launches Rosetta, the first spacecraft to make a soft landing on a comet; 67P/Churyumov-Gerasimenko.

2015 – 10TH AUGUST

The first food eaten and grown in space is lettuce on board the International Space Station.

MAIN IMAGE: International Space Station

A BRIEF HISTORY OF

SPACE EXPLORATION

Although many scientists such as Robert Esnault Pelterie in France and Eugen Sänger in Austria undertook experiments and wrote theories on rocketry and space travel, three men in particular are considered to be the fathers of space travel.

In 1883, the Russian mathematician and schoolteacher Konstantine Tsiolkovsky was hard at work studying the theory of motion by a rocket. By 1896, having developed a rigorous theory of rocket propulsion, he was investigating the possibilities for an all-metal balloon, streamlined aeroplanes and trains and rockets capable of inter-planetary travel. Having developed an aerodynamics laboratory, he then constructed a wind tunnel and carried out experiments with spheres cylinders, cones and other objects. Based on his concept of an all-metal dirigible (an airship), he constructed a model, but financial support was not forthcoming.

In 1894 he wrote an article about an aeroplane, a birdlike flying machine and drew a monoplane. In 1903, his most important work, an article entitled "*Exploration of cosmic space by means of reaction devices*", set out to prove that a rocket could be sent into space. He is considered to be the first theorist and advocate for human flight in space, and a champion of the idea that life is not restricted to our own planet.

Scepticism about his ideas prevented him from being able to build a rocket, but his studies and work were of enormous influence in rocket research in the 20th century.

Nine years before Tsiolkovsky's death, an American, Robert Hutchings Goddard, an engineer, physicist, professor and inventor, launched the world's first liquid-fuelled rocket. It was the 16th of March 1926; the space age had begun.

It was H. G. Wells classic science fiction novel The War of the Worlds,

RIGHT: Dr. Robert H. Goddard at a blackboard at Clark University in Worcester, Massachusetts, in 1924. Goddard began teaching physics in 1914 at Clark and in 1923 was named the Director of the Physical Laboratory

BELOW L-R: Robert Esnault Pelterie | Eugen Sänger on the left | Konstantine Tsiolkovsky with airship models

Moon
limit of balloon; 20 miles
limit of atmosphere;
200 miles
6 miles/s
1 lb
ARTH

which Goddard had read when he was 16 years old that inflamed the young man's mind with the wonders of spaceflight. He was still an undergraduate when he wrote a method whereby gyro stabilisation would balance aeroplanes, and by 1912, he was calculating the flight paths and velocities of rockets. Working for Clark University, he launched powder rockets in 1915. As the rockets only converted some 2% of their fuel into thrust, he then used nozzles; to dramatic effect.

As his work became more complicated, he applied to the Smithsonian for a grant, which was awarded to him in the sum of $5000. He began experimenting with liquid-fuel rockets in 1921, and only five years later was ready for his test flight using gasoline and liquid oxygen as fuel. It rose just 41 feet during a 2.5-second flight and landed in a cabbage field; but the first step had been made. His enthusiastic friend Charles Lindbergh secured Goddard financial support from the financier Daniel Guggenheim. Nonetheless, progress in United States was slow and interest was lukewarm at best. Ominously, it was the rocket developers in Germany who took the greatest interest in his work.

Goddard persevered, and by 1935 he had sent another rocket with a gyroscopic guidance system 4800 feet into the air at almost 550 mph.

Shortly before the end of World War II, Goddard and his team had put together the basic control system for rocket plane propulsion.

Goddard died in 1945, but his inspiring words are another of his legacies: in 1933, he said that under no circumstances "*must we allow ourselves to be deterred from the achievement of space travel, test by test and step by step, until one day we succeed, cost what it may*".

RIGHT: Colourized image of Dr. Robert H. Goddard and a liquid oxygen-gasoline rocket at Auburn, Massachusetts

TOP RIGHT: Robert Hutchings at Clark University, Massachusetts

BOTTOM RIGHT: Hermann Oberth (forefront) with officials of the Army Ballistic Missile Agency at Huntsville, Alabama, 1956. L-R around Oberth: 1) Dr. Ernst Stuhlinger (seated). 2) Major General H.N. Toftoy, Commanding Officer and person responsible for "Project Paperclip," which took scientists and engineers out of Germany after World War II to design rockets for American military use. 3) Dr. Wernher von Braun, Director, Development Operations Division. 4) Dr. Robert Lusser, a Project Paperclip engineer

At around the same time as Goddard was delving into the wonders of rocket technology in the US, in Europe another pioneer of space travel was also trying to unravel the technical difficulties surrounding rocket-powered space travel. Hermann Oberth was a German national of Romanian birth and another man who had been enthused an author, this time by Jules Verne. He took to the study of interplanetary travel with single-minded dedication and delivered his doctoral thesis in 1922 on rocket-powered flight. Oberth met with the same initial official reaction as Goddard; rejection. But his revenge came one year later with his book The Rocket into Interplanetary Space — an explanation of the mathematical theory of rocketry and a discourse on space travel and the construction of a space station — which became a classic and brought the recognition he deserved.

Oberth's publications inspired others to form rocket clubs in Germany — one of them harboured a young Wernher von Braun, later one of Germany's foremost aerospace engineers, who helped develop the German V-2 rocket, and who later became the father of rocket technology in the US; Oberth became his mentor.

Oberth's first rocket was launched on May the 7th 1932 not far from Berlin.

Oberth lived long enough to be see the era of space

LEFT: Researcher Robert Miller led an investigation into the combustor performance of a German Jumo 004 engine at the National Advisory Committee for Aeronautics (NACA) Lewis Flight Propulsion Laboratory. The setup in this photograph was created for a tour of NACA Lewis by members of the Institute of Aeronautical Science on March 22, 1945

ABOVE: Dr. Wernher von Braun is shown in this photograph from 1961 with members of his management team. Pictured from left to right are, Werner Kuers, Director of the Manufacturing Engineering Division; Dr. Walter Haeussermann, Director of the Astrionics Division; Dr. William Mrazek, Propulsion and Vehicle Engineering Division; Dr. von Braun; Dieter Grau, Director of the Quality Assurance Division; Dr. Oswald Lange, Director of the Saturn Systems Office; and Erich Neubert, Associate Deputy Director for Research and Development

THE EARLY YEARS

Space exploration came of age when the world was writhing in the turmoil of WWII. The Nazis had understood the benefits of rocket technology as a weapon of conflict, and Wernher von Braun was engaged as chief engineer in the project that gave birth to the first rocket-powered flight by the V-2, launched in 1942. When the war ended, Braun and his team together with their blueprints were encouraged to go to America to continue their work on space rockets for the Americans.

Other German engineers had gone to post-war Russia, although their role in soviet rocket development was limited, and by the mid 1950s they had returned home.

Soviet technology had also made considerable progress, and on the 17th of August 1933, the first liquid-fuelled rocket was launched. Later, the Rocket Propulsion Research Institute (RNII) was formed under the auspices of the military; this organisation would later play a central role in Soviet technological achievement in the field of space exploration. Soviet head of state Joseph Stalin was a late convert to rocket technology and having arrested the man known in the Soviet Union as the father of practical astronautics, rocket engineer Sergey Korolyov in 1937 as part of his 5-year purge of intellectuals, later realised his mistake when WWII started. For most of the war years, Korolyov was permitted to work in a design bureau in prison, where he worked on weapons technology, and at the war's end, he was part of a team sent to examine the V-2 rocket.

With the help of those German teams, the Soviets were able to launch sub-orbital V-2 rockets in 1947 in a program that included radiation and animal experiments on some of the flights.

In wartime America, in the meantime, men such as Frank Malina

RIGHT: Wernher von Braun

BELOW L-R: Army Research Station, rocket experimental area. V2 rocket (unit 4) on launch pad | Sergei Korolyov, 1966 | Twelve scientific specialists of the Peenemuende team, They led the Army's space efforts at ABMA before transfer of the team to National Aeronautic and Space Administration (NASA)

were working in the California Institute of Technology working on aeronautical projects alongside a man who later went home to become one of China's foremost rocket scientists; Qian Xuesen. The men at CIT formed JPL, the Jet Propulsion Laboratory, and developed weapons for the US military.

Post WWII, their work was channelled into space experiments, and JPL was absorbed into a new organisation, NASA, the National Aeronautics and Space Administration, formed in 1958, ostensibly for non-military space exploration.

Also with the help of the Germans, the Americans now conducted their own test firings, which took place between 1946 and 1951 at White Sands in New Mexico, now known as the "*Birthplace of America's Missile and Space Activity*".

Although WAC Corporals were used in the first tests, they were under-powered, so JPL engineers used a solid-fuel rocket booster, which they dubbed "*Tiny Tim*", to get the rocket out of its launch tower and up to speed. The booster generated 50,000 pounds of thrust for one half second. As the WAC Corporal left its 100-foot launch tower its speed was almost 275 mph.

But it was the 46-foot tall V-2 rockets that soon took over the show; they could exceed altitudes of 100 miles with a launch weight of 28,000 pounds. When launched in April 1946, it disintegrated into a huge fireball at 3.5 miles. On May the 10th, the first successful launch took place.

Fortunately, despite the primary purpose of the tests being to advance rocket technology, the military had the foresight to direct that all V-2s carry some sort of scientific payload. The "*V-2 Upper-Atmosphere Research Panel*" was created to take proposals for experiments and decide which agency would use each rocket.

MAIN IMAGE: X-15 launch techniques were investigated using on-twentieth scale models mounted in the 7x10 FT Tunnel, 1959

On July the 9th and 19th 1946, V-2s carried corn seeds and fruit flies aloft to expose them to cosmic radiation. Other studies included solar spectroscopy, solar radiation, artificial meteorites, temperatures, ambient pressures, winds and the composition of the atmosphere itself at various altitudes.

Scientists were keen to join forces in space exploration, and in the 1950s they planned the International Geophysical year, the IGY, and sent a satellite into orbit between July 1957 and December 1958. One reason the US government supported the IGY satellite program was to establish the principle that outer space would not be considered the territorial sovereignty of any single nation and that an orbiting satellite was free to roam wherever it was sent, an essential rule if satellites were to gather reconnaissance intelligence. Satellites equipped with cameras that could fly over Soviet territory were an attractive proposition to the US military. However, the Russians launched their own satellite in October 1975, Sputnik 1, the first artificial satellite, which produced a crisis in the American psyche, a "*Pearl Harbor*" effect on American public opinion, creating an illusion of a technological gap.

Sputnik was sent up on the 4th of October 1957 and orbited for three weeks. When its batteries died, it continued to orbit silently for two months before falling back into the atmosphere. Sputnik 1's polished metal sphere was 58 cm (23 in) in diameter with four external radio antennas that broadcast radio pulses. The space race was truly underway.

LATER IN 1957 SPUTNIK 2 WAS IN SPACE WITH LAIKA THE DOG.

The British Interplanetary Society had been promoting the concept of human space since the 1930s, and in the 1950s, feature films were bringing the idea to widespread attention; Destination Moon

MAIN IMAGE: Sputnik 2

BELOW L-R: Exploded view into Sputnik 1 interior | Mock-up of Laika in position | Laika

OPP. PAGE L-R: JFK giving his famous speach | A three-year-old chimpanzee, named Ham, in the biopack couch for the MR-2 suborbital test flight. On January 31, 1961

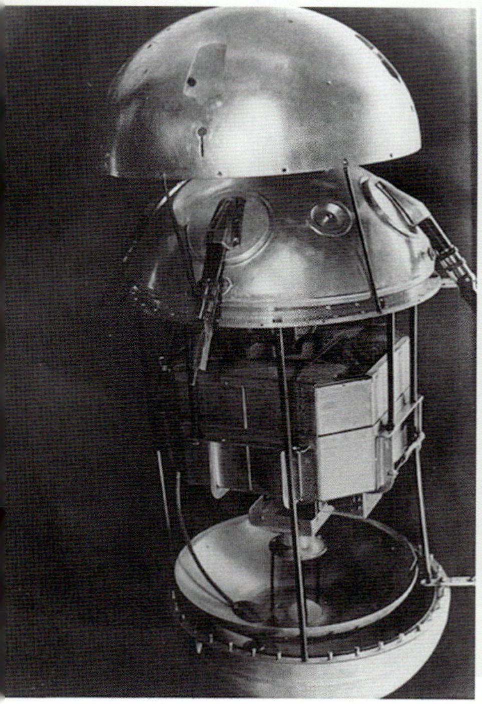

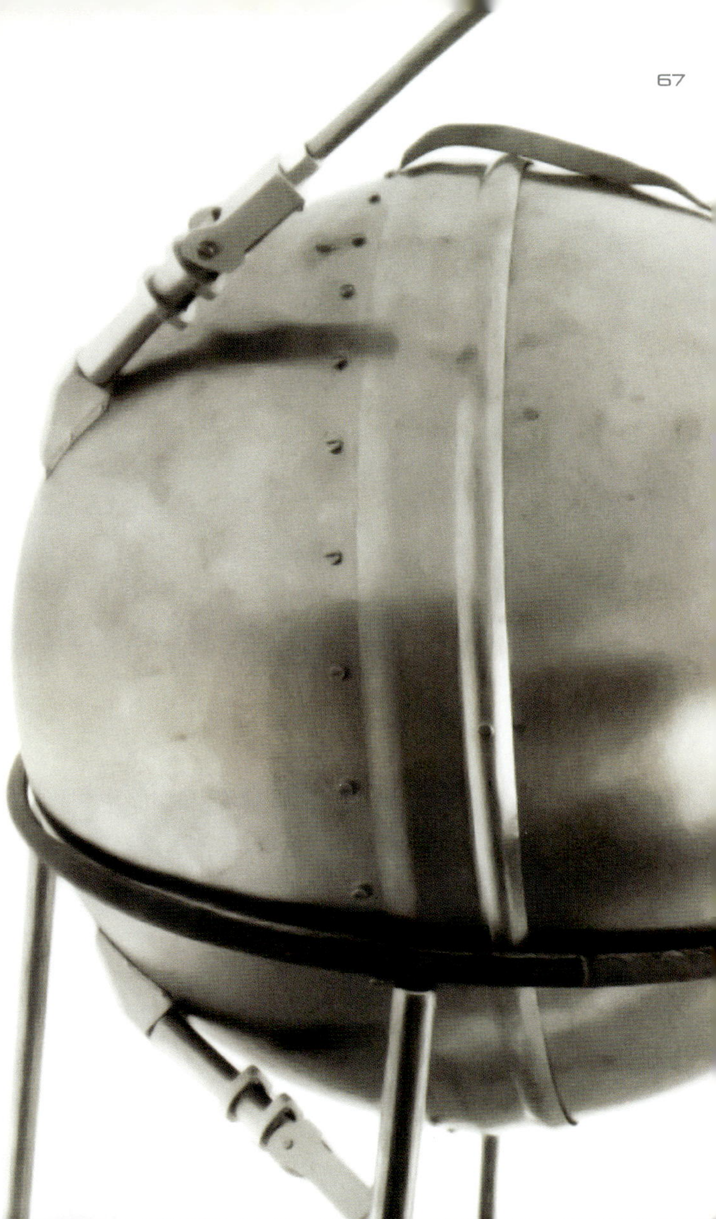

and The Day the Earth Stood Still, or When Worlds Collide brought the idea of human space travel to life. Unidentified Flying Objects, UFOs, thought to be alien spacecraft, could now be seen in the sky; at least by some people. Science-fiction authors Arthur C. Clarke and Isaac Asimov were also involved in public debate on the subject and expounded their theories in their novels.

The Russians were once again ahead of the Americans when on the 12th of April 1961, the Vostok 1 was sent into space and the history books by carrying Yuri Gagarin onboard, the first human in space; the dream had come true. The final frontier was open for business.

By 1961, NASA had also advanced its human spaceflight program, Project Mercury, and on May the 5th that year, Alan B. Shepard Jr. became the first American to fly into space when he rode in his Mercury capsule on a 15-minute suborbital mission.

Project Apollo was given priority at NASA on May the 25th 1961, when President John F. Kennedy announced: "*I believe that this nation should commit itself to achieving the goal, before this decade*

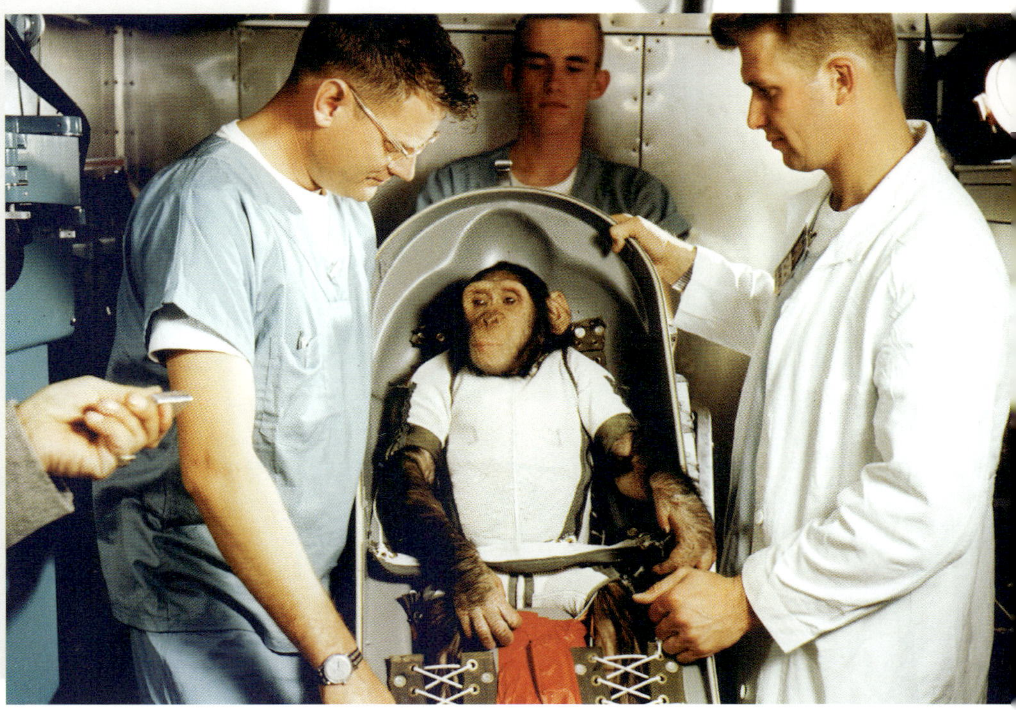

OPP PAGE: Fisheye view of astronauts James A. McDivitt and Edward H. White II inside the Gemini-4 spacecraft during simulated exercises at pad 19, Cape Kennedy, Florida

LEFT: The Gemini-Titan 4 (GT-4) spaceflight launches from Cape Kennedy's Pad 19 at 10:16 a.m. (EST) on June 3, 1965. The GT-4 spacecraft carried astronauts James A. McDivitt, command pilot, and Edward H. White II, pilot, on a four-day, 62-revolution mission

is out, of landing a man on the Moon and returning him safely to Earth." This statement was in direct response to Soviet successes in space, and the Apollo program was employed in the space race as a high-profile effort for the US to try and demonstrate to the world its scientific and technological superiority over its cold-war rival.

One year later, John H. Glenn Jr. became the first US astronaut to orbit the Earth; it was February the 20th 1962. With six flights, Project Mercury had achieved its goal of putting piloted spacecraft into an Earth orbit and retrieving the astronauts safely. Emboldened by Mercury's success, project Gemini was born to exploit Mercury's achievements, and NASA's human spaceflight program became more ambitious; a spacecraft would be built to house two astronauts. The ten flights undertaken by the Gemini craft also provided NASA scientists and engineers with more data on weightlessness, perfected re-entry and splashdown procedures and demonstrated how to rendezvous and dock in space. The theories were put into successful practice; on June the 3rd 1965, Edward H. White, Jr., became the first US astronaut to conduct a spacewalk.

By then though, the Russians had once again stolen a march on the US by launching Vostok 6 on June the 16th 1963. On board

was Valentina Tereshkova, the first woman in space. Her training had included rocket theory, spacecraft engineering, weightless flights, isolation tests, centrifuge tests, pilot training in jet planes and 120 parachute jumps. Logging more flight time than the combined times of all American astronauts up to that date, she maintained a flight log and photographed the horizon, images which later helped identify atmospheric aerosol layers.

Then Russia's Luna 10 became the first artificial satellite of the moon in 1966, (following on from Luna 9, which had been the first automatic landing on another celestial body). Carrying such scientific instruments as a gamma-ray spectrometer, a triaxial magnetometer and a meteorite detector, once in lunar orbit, Luna 10 gathered important data on the strength of the moon's magnetic field, its radiation belts, and the nature of lunar rocks.

America had been busy, too, pouring billions into the Apollo project, and not even a tragedy could be allowed to stop the relentless march of space exploration. On January the 27th 1967, a fire broke out in an Apollo capsule on the ground claiming the lives of astronauts Roger B. Chaffee, Virgil "*Gus*" Grissom, and Edward H. White Jr.

1967 turned out to be a year of tragedy in space exploration, for the Russians then had to watch their own disaster unfold. On April the 23rd 1967, two years after the last human flight, the Soviet Union launched a new generation of spacecraft; the Soyuz 1 was sent into space with veteran cosmonaut Vladimir Komarov on board to practice a space rendezvous with a second Soyuz.

But one of the craft's solar arrays failed to open properly, which deprived Komarov of over half of his power supply. The mission would be cut short.

A backup telemetry antenna also failed. The likely outcome of

OPP. PAGE: Edward H. White II, pilot on the Gemini-Titan 4 spaceflight, shown during his egress from the spacecraft. A shaded visor protects him from the unfiltered rays of the sun. The first American astronaut to walk in space. He was outside for 21 minutes during the third revolution of the Gemini-4 mission

BELOW L-R: Virgil "Gus" Grissom | Edward H. White Jr. | Roger B. Chaffee

ABOVE: The ascent stage of Eagle just prior to its rendezvous with the Command Module, 1969

RIGHT: 'The Eagle has landed'

this would have been sporadic reception. Combined with glitches in other sensors this meant that the cosmonaut could not even control his orientation effectively. Docking was out of the question. Also, only one solar array "*wing*" had deployed so Soyuz 1's shape was now asymmetrical; orientation would be even more difficult. To provide greater aerodynamic "*lift*" during re-entry, the Soyuz's non-spherical descent module base had been flattened, and it also had an offset centre of gravity. At one point, Komarov knocked his boots on the side of the spacecraft in an attempt to release the deployment mechanism for the solar array.

A RETRO RE-ATTEMPT FAILED.

By now it seemed that Komarov realised that he was unlikely to survive re-entry. He spoke to Soviet Premier Alexei Kosygin, and to his own wife, Valentina, telling her how to deal with his affairs and how she should help their children.

Nonetheless, re-entry was achieved and despite the 8G load imposed by the steep, ballistic descent, Komarov might still have landed safely. A drogue chute was deployed successfully, but failed to pull the main canopy from its storage canister. The reserve parachute was jettisoned. It failed to open when it became entangled with the cords of the drogue.

Soyuz 1 struck the ground at 640 km/h. Komarov was killed instantly, and the solid-fuel rockets exploded sending an inferno of flame through the craft.

Recovering from its own disaster, America finally achieved a major 'first' in the battle for space supremacy: It was July the 20th 1969, and Neil A. Armstrong dramatically piloted the lunar module to the lunar surface with less than 30 seconds worth of fuel remaining. He told Earth, "*That's one small step for man, one giant leap for*

LEFT: Edwin E. Aldrin Jr. on the surface of the moon

BELOW L-R: This is the seventh of 25 images captured by the crew in attempt to provide a 360 degree Lunar surface scene | Posed photograph beside the deployed United States flag during an Apollo 11 extravehicular activity (EVA) on the lunar surface | Footprint in the moons surface

OPP. PAGE: This view of Earth showing clouds over its surface was photographed from the Apollo 11 spacecraft during its translunar journey toward the moon. The spacecraft was already about 10,000 nautical miles from Earth when this picture was taken

LEFT: Astronaut Edwin E. Aldrin Jr., lunar module pilot, prepares to deploy the Early Apollo Scientific Experiments Package (EASEP) on the surface of the moon during the Apollo 11 extravehicular activity

ABOVE: The LM landed on the moon's surface on July 20, 1969 in the region known as Mare Tranquilitatis (the Sea of Tranquility). Shown here is Aldrin Jr. making his exit from the LM to the lunar surface. Armstrong, who was already on the surface, took this photograph

ABOVE: High-angle view at Launch Complex 39, Kennedy Space Center (KSC), showing the Apollo 12

RIGHT: Sitting in the life raft, during the Apollo 12 Pacific recovery, are the three mission astronauts; Alan L. Bean, pilot of the Lunar Module (LM), Intrepid; Richard Gordon, pilot of the Command Module (CM), Yankee Clipper; and Spacecraft Commander Charles Conrad

315
NAVY

mankind"; the Apollo 11 mission had fulfilled Kennedy's challenge by successfully landing Armstrong and Edwin E. "*Buzz*" Aldrin Jr. on the surface of the moon. After taking soil samples, photographs and doing other tasks on the moon, Armstrong and Aldrin rendezvoused with their colleague Michael Collins in lunar orbit for a safe voyage back to Earth.

NASA conducted another five successful lunar landing missions, although the Apollo 13 mission in April 1970 gave NASA a fright when astronauts and ground crews had to improvise to end the mission safely after an oxygen tank burst midway through the journey to the moon. Even though the mission never landed on the moon, it did confirm that NASA had the ability to adapt to the unforeseen technical difficulties inherent in human spaceflight.

The cold war thawed a little, in space at least, when in 1975 NASA co-operated with the Soviet Union to achieve the first international human spaceflight, the Apollo-Soyuz Test Project (ASTP). This project successfully tested joint rendezvous and docking procedures for spacecraft from the US and the USSR. After being launched separately from their respective countries, the Apollo and Soyuz crews met in space and conducted various experiments for two days.

The US then embarked on the Space Shuttle project sending the first one into space in April 1981, and two years later, on June the 18th 1983, Sally Ride lifted off to become the first American woman to make the trip out into the darkness — but mission control could only watch helplessly as on January the 28th 1986, one of the boosters on the Challenger leaked causing the main liquid fuel tank to explode 73 seconds after launch; all 7 crew members were killed. The Shuttle program was grounded for over two years, while NASA and its contractors worked to redesign the Solid Rocket Boosters and implement management reforms to increase safety. On September the 29th 1988, the Shuttle successfully returned to flight and NASA then flew a total of 87 successful missions.

Because Earth's atmosphere alters and blocks the light that comes from space, it became important to send a telescope up above Earth's atmosphere and therefore provide a better view of the universe than telescopes have at ground level. The Hubble Space Telescope was the answer to the problem, and it was deployed from the cargo bay of the Space Shuttle Discovery on April the 25th 1990 as part of STS-31.

(Hubble is named after Edwin P. Hubble, who made important discoveries in the early 1900s, showing that the galaxy containing the solar system – the Milky Way – was only one of many galaxies. His work helped show that the universe is expanding. This led to the big-bang theory, which says that the universe began with an intense burst of energy and has been expanding ever since.)

MAIN IMAGE: Clouds over the Atlantic Ocean serve as the backdrop for this 70mm scene of the Atmospheric Laboratory for Applications and Science (ATLAS-3) payload in the cargo bay of the Earth-orbiting Space Shuttle Atlantis

OPP. PAGE L-R: Extravehicular activity (EVA) photographed with a camera affixed to the gear of astronaut Bruce McCandless II. The mission specialist was equipped with the nitrogen-propelled, hand-controlled Manned Maneuvering Unit (MMU), which took him some 90 meters away from the Space Shuttle Challenger | The space shuttle Challenger lifted off from Pad 39B Jan. 28, 1986 | The Challenger explodes

JPL
NASA

Another thaw in Russian-American relationships began in 1993 when the two countries joined with other nations to build a joint facility that became known as the International Space Station, (ISS). To prepare for building the ISS starting in late 1998, NASA participated in a series of Shuttle missions to the Russian station Mir, and seven American astronauts lived aboard Mir for extended stays. Permanent habitation of the ISS began with the launch of the Expedition 1 crew on October the 31st, and the docking on November the 2nd 2000.

But the life of pioneers in any era has been fraught with dangers, and on February the 1st 2003, as the Columbia orbiter was returning to Earth on the STS-107 mission, it disintegrated about 15 minutes before it was due to have landed. Commander John Young and his six crew lost their lives. Columbia had seen 22 years of service and over 27 missions. The Columbia Accident Investigation Board was quickly formed and determined that a small piece of foam had come off the external tank and had struck the reinforced carbon panels on the underside of the left wing during the launch on January the 16th. When the orbiter was returning to Earth, the breach in the RCC panels allowed hot gas to penetrate the orbiter, leading to a catastrophic failure.

A year of tragedy for the US, but a year of triumph for China. On the 15th of October 2003, the country launched a person into space for the first time, 42 years after the launch of Vostok 1, with the flight of Shenzou 5 carrying Yang Liwei on board.

One of the most exciting projects for the near future will be a trip to the sun. Earth is bombarded by solar wind every day, but exactly where the particles are created or how they are accelerated is unknown. Two missions are planned.

MAIN IMAGE: The Hubble Space Telescope, in the grasp of Discovery's remote manipulator system, is backdropped over Earth, 332 nautical miles below

BELOW LEFT: Astrotech processing facility in Titusville, Florida, technicians and engineers deploy the magnetometer boom on NASA's Parker Solar Probe

BELOW RIGHT: The second stage of a United Launch Alliance Delta IV Heavy is being mated to the common booster core inside the Horizontal Integration Facility near Space Launch Complex 37 at Cape Canaveral Air Force Station in Florida

The first of these is NASA's Parker Solar Probe. The spaceship will fly to within 3.9 million miles of the sun's surface, closer than has ever been attempted. The mission is named after the astrophysicist Eugene Parker, who first put forward the theory of solar wind.

After the launch of Parker, Europe will be close behind, launching their own mission to study the sun; carrying ten instruments, the Solar Orbiter will study the sun's surface, investigate solar wind flows and the causes for the 11-year solar cycle.

These flights will be accompanied by more US and European spacecraft with NASA sending TESS (Transiting Exoplanet Survey Satellite) to search space for exoplanets and ESAs space telescope CHEOPS (Characterising Exoplanets Satellite) engaged in the same mission objectives.

And while Solar Orbiter and Solar Probe are heating up, Japan's JAXA's Hayabusa 2, which was launched in December 2014 by the Japanese space agency, is expected to stay around an asteroid for eighteen months, before leaving in 2019 and arriving back at Earth around the end of 2020.

Space exploration has accomplished many great scientific and technological feats. The technology used has been adapted for many non-aerospace uses by industry and in civilian life. Yet, perhaps more importantly, our exploration of space has taught us to view the Earth, ourselves, and the universe in a new way. While the tremendous technical and scientific accomplishments involved demonstrate vividly that humans can achieve previously inconceivable feats, it should also be humbling to us all to realise that our beautiful Earth is just a tiny "*blue marble*" in the immensity of the cosmos.

MAIN IMAGE: First stage of a United Launch Alliance Delta IV Heavy rocket is at the Vertical Integration Facility near Space Launch Complex 37 at Cape Canaveral, Florida.

BELOW LEFT: A SpaceX Falcon 9 rocket lifts off from Space Launch Complex 40 at Cape Canaveral Air Force Station in Florida, carrying NASA's Transiting Exoplanet Survey Satellite (TESS)

BELOW RIGHT: Artist concept of Hayabusa 2

NASA

TOP: Backdropped against a blue and white Earth, the Space Shuttle Orbiter Atlantis was photographed by an Expedition 5 crew member onboard the International Space Station

ABOVE: Docked to the International Space Station (ISS), a Soyuz vehicle (foreground) and the Space Shuttle Atlantis were photographed by a crew member in the Pirs docking compartment on the orbital outpost

LEFT: Atop the massive mobile launcher platform and crawler-transporter, Space Shuttle Atlantis begins rolling through the open door of the Vehicle Assembly Building for the journey to Launch Pad 39A

TOP: Space Shuttle Orbiter Endeavor Launches to deliver the Expedition Six Crew to the ISS, the return of Expedition Five crew back to Earth, and the installation and activation of the Port 1 Integrated Truss Assembly (P1)

ABOVE: Susan J. Helms works outside the International Space Station while holding onto a rigid umbilical and her feet anchored to the Remote Manipulator System robotic arm on the Space Shuttle Discovery

RIGHT: International Space Station, separated from the Space Shuttle Discovery after several days of joint activities and an important crew exchange. This photograph was taken by one of the crew of this mission from the aft flight deck of Discovery.

RIGHT: In the grasp of the Shuttle's Remote Manipulator System (RMS) robot arm, the U.S. Laboratory, Destiny, is moved from its stowage position in the cargo bay of the Space Shuttle Atlantis. This photograph was taken by astronaut Thomas D. Jones during his Extravehicular Activity (EVA). The American-made Destiny module is the cornerstone for space-based research aboard the orbiting platform and the centerpiece of the International Space Station

OPP. PAGE: Anchored to a foot restraint on the Space Station Remote Manipulator System (SSRMS) or Canadarm2, astronaut David A. Wolf, STS-112 mission specialist, participates in the mission's first session of extravehicular activity (EVA). Wolf is carrying the Starboard One (S1) outboard nadir external camera which was installed on the end of the S1 Truss on the International Space Station

A BRIEF EXPLANATION OF OUR

SOLAR SYSTEM

PLUTO

2003 UB_{313}

PLANETS

DWARF PLANETS

the pressure in the core was so great that hydrogen atoms began to combine and form helium, releasing a tremendous amount of energy. With that, our sun was born, and it eventually amassed more than 99 percent of the available matter.

Matter farther out in the disk was also clumping together. These clumps smashed into one another, forming larger and larger objects. Some of them grew big enough for their gravity to shape them into spheres, becoming planets, dwarf planets and large moons. In other cases, planets did not form: the asteroid belt is made of bits and pieces of the early solar system that could never quite come together into a planet. Other smaller leftover pieces became asteroids, comets, meteoroids, and small, irregular moons. Nearest the sun, only rocky material could withstand the heat when the solar system was young. For this reason, the first four planets – Mercury, Venus, Earth and Mars – are terrestrial planets; they're small with solid, rocky surfaces.

Meanwhile, materials we are used to seeing as ice, liquid or gas settled in the outer regions of the young solar system. Gravity pulled these materials together, and that is where we find gas giants Jupiter and Saturn and ice giants Uranus and Neptune.

There are more than 150 known moons in our solar system, and of the eight planets, Mercury and Venus are the only ones with no moons. The giant planets grab the most moons. Jupiter and Saturn have long led our solar system's moon counts. Pluto, smaller than our own moon, has five moons in its orbit, including the Charon, a moon so large it makes Pluto wobble.

OUR SOLAR SYSTEM

SUN

MERCURY

VENUS

EARTH

MARS

ASTEROIDS

JUPITER

SATURN

URANUS

NEPTUNE

PLUTO

DWARF PLANETS

KUIPER BELT

OORT CLOUD

Mercury, Venus, Earth and Mars, the inner solar system planets, are all terrestrial planets; in other words they are composed of silicate rock and minerals that are differentiated between a metallic core and a silicate mantle and crust. (At the Earth's centre is the core, which has two parts; the solid, inner core of iron has a radius of about 760 miles (about 1,220 km), according to NASA. It is surrounded by a liquid outer core composed of a nickel-iron alloy. The outer core is about 1,355 miles (2,180 km) thick. The inner core spins at a different speed than the rest of the planet. This is thought to cause Earth's magnetic field. The mantle under the crust is about 1,800 miles deep (2,890 km). It's composed mostly of silicate rocks rich in magnesium and iron. Intense heat causes the rocks to rise before they then cool and sink back down to the core. The crust is divided into huge plates that float on the mantle, the next layer. The plates are constantly in motion; they move at about the same rate as a growing fingernail.

Our Solar system contains 779,000,944 asteroids; 3,521 comets; 8 planets; 9 dwarf planets; 188 known natural satellites known as moons. Over 200 minor-planet moons have been observed. Earth has one moon which is 0.273 times the size of Earth, Mars has two, the larger one is Phobos, 22.7 kilometres in diameter, and Deimos. Jupiter has 69 moons, Saturn 62 and Uranus 27.

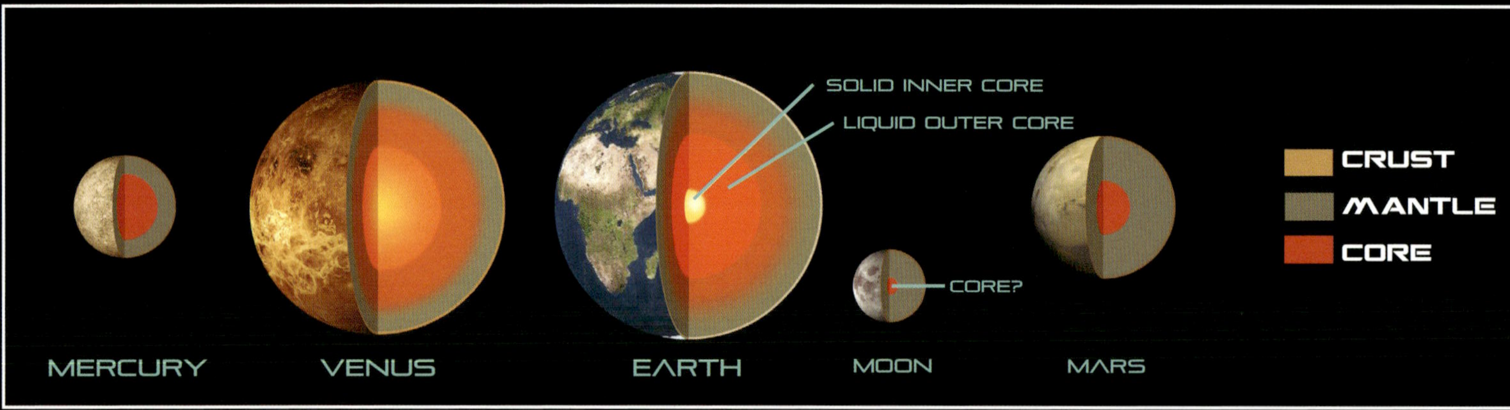

MAIN IMAGE: Asteroid 243 Ida is a mosaic of five image frames acquired by NASA's Galileo spacecraft solid-state imaging system at ranges of 3,057 to 3,821 kilometers (1,900 to 2,375 miles) on August 28, 1993

RIGHT L-R: On December 16, 1992, 8 days after its encounter with Earth, the Galileo spacecraft looked back from a distance of about 6.2 million kilometers (3.9 million miles) to capture this remarkable view of the Moon in orbit about Earth | The High Resolution Imaging Science Experiment HiRISE camera on NASA Mars Reconnaissance Orbiter took two images of the larger of Mars two moons, Phobos | Color-enhanced views of Deimos, Mars' other moon | The Red Planet is home to Valles Marineris, the solar system's largest canyon. Within this canyon lies Ius Chasma. This image, which spans the floor of its southern trench, was taken by the Mars Reconnaissance Orbiter. The canyon is well-known for its fine stratigraphic layers modified by wind and water

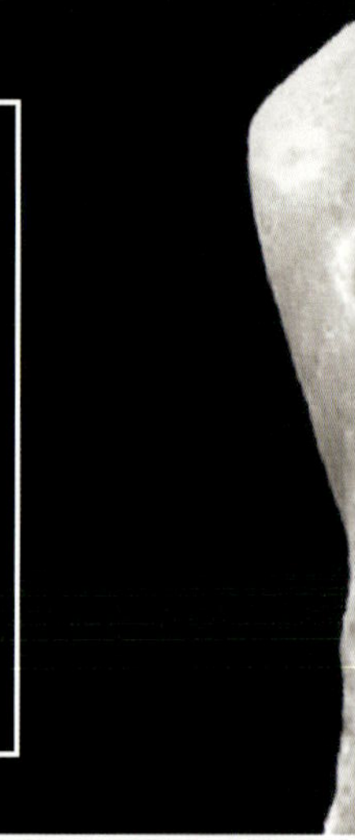

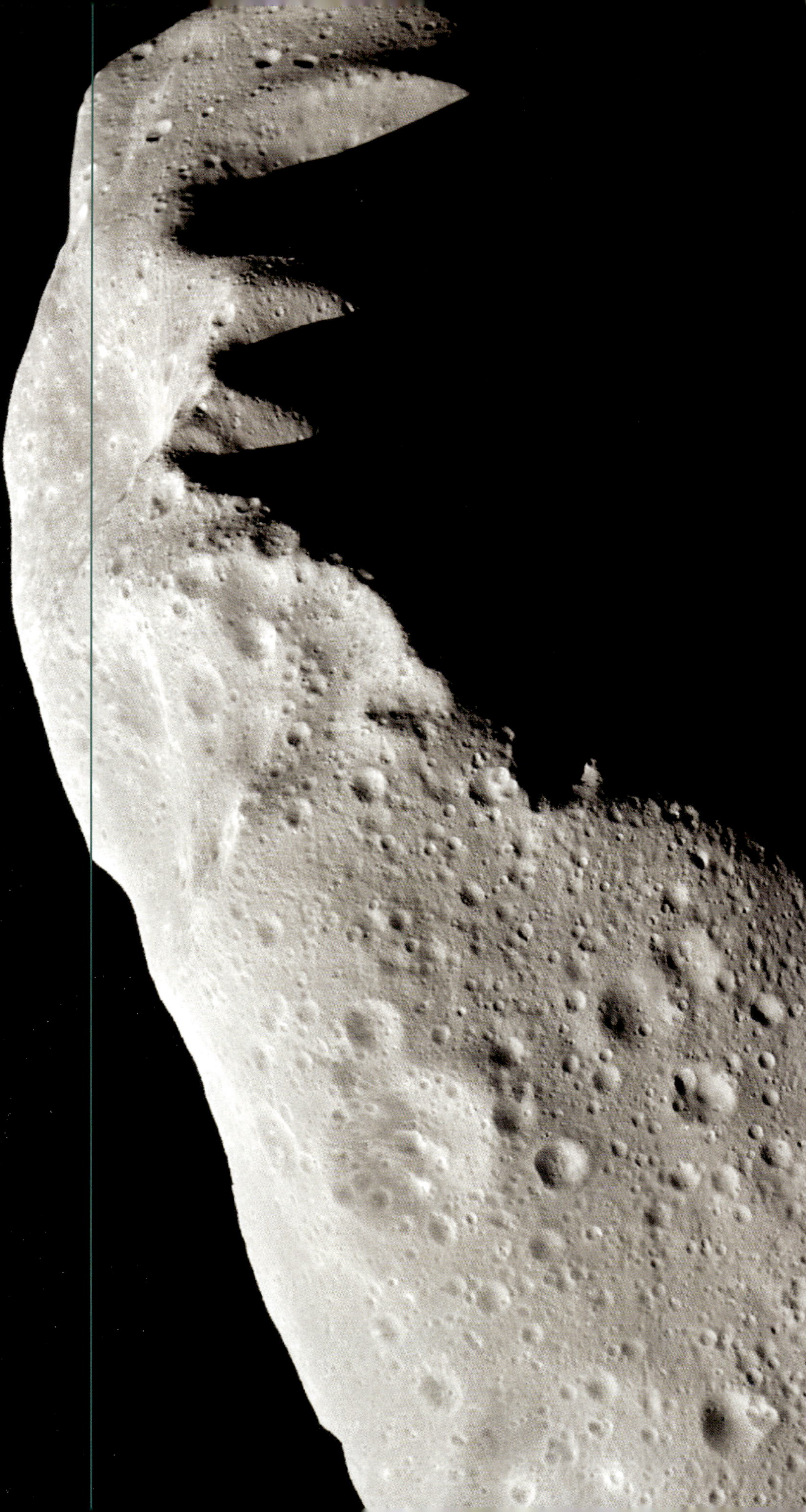

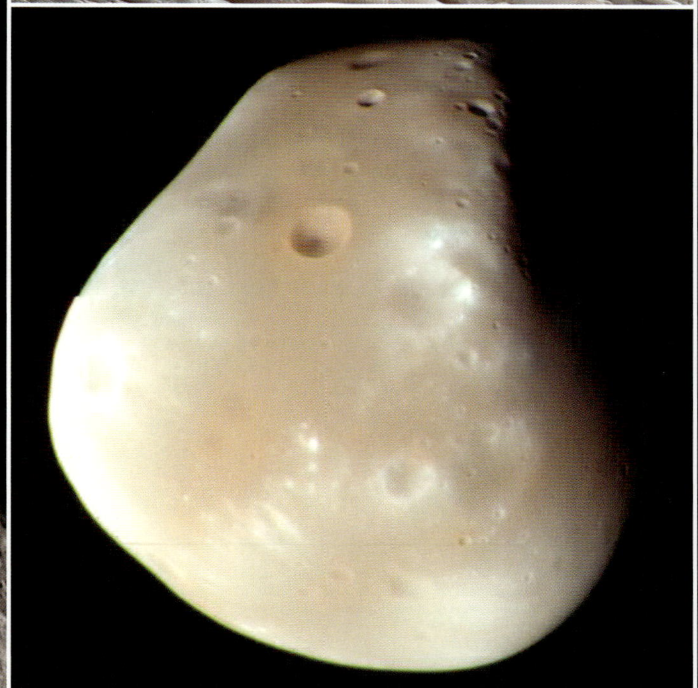

TOP: The Hubble Space Telescope in a picture snapped by a Servicing Mission 4 crewmember just after the Space Shuttle Atlantis captured Hubble with its robotic arm on May 13, 2009, beginning the mission to upgrade and repair the telescope

ABOVE: This image shows a composite view of the Crab Nebula, an iconic supernova remnant in our Milky Way galaxy, as viewed by the Herschel Space Observatory and the Hubble Space Telescope

RIGHT: This Hubble image of the Bubble Nebula, or NGC 7635, was chosen to mark the 26th anniversary of the launch of Hubble into Earth orbit by the STS-31 space shuttle crew on April 24, 1990

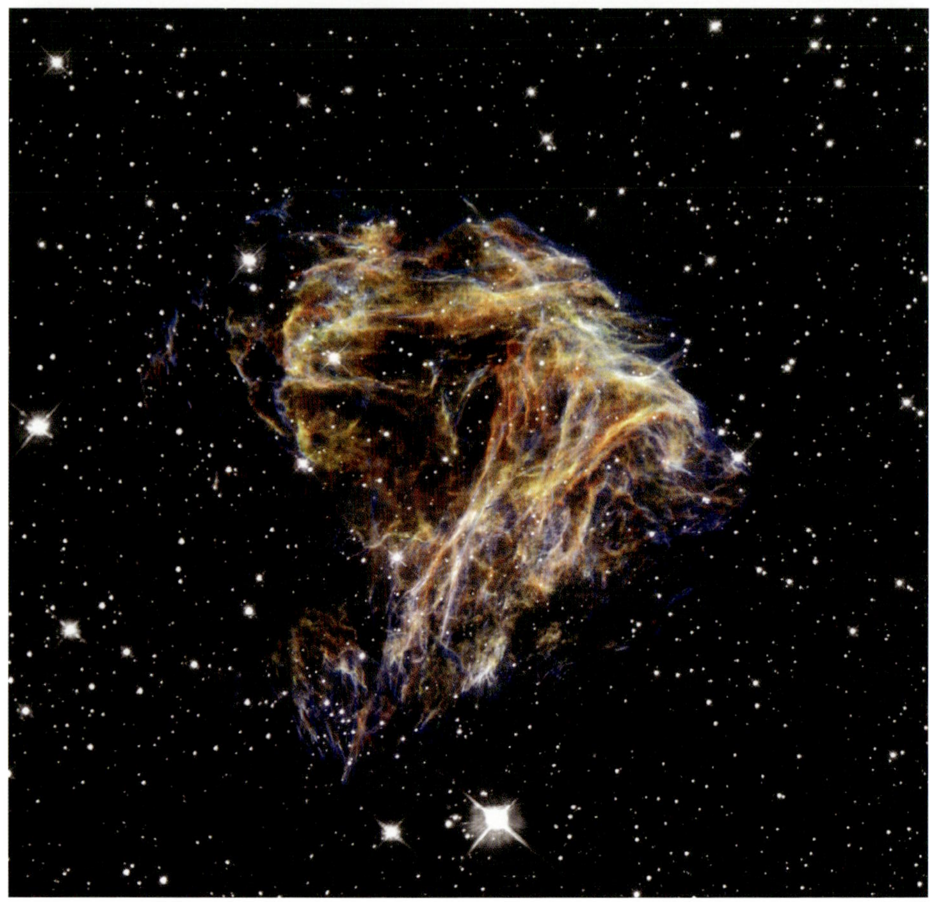

ABOVE: The Crab Nebula is one of the most intricately structured and highly dynamical objects ever observed. The new Hubble image of the Crab was assembled from 24 individual exposures taken with the NASA/ESA Hubble Space Telescope

TOP RIGHT: NASA Hubble Space Telescope captures the chaotic activity atop a three-light-year-tall pillar of gas and dust that is being eaten away by the brilliant light from nearby bright stars in a tempestuous stellar nursery called the Carina Nebula.

BOTTOM RIGHT: Resembling sparks from a fireworks display, this image taken by a JPL camera onboard NASA Hubble Space Telescope shows delicate filaments that are sheets of debris from a stellar explosion in the nearby Large Magellanic Cloud galaxy.

OPP. PAGE: This majestic view taken by NASA Spitzer Space Telescope tells an untold story of life and death in the Eagle nebula, an industrious star-making factory located 7,000 light-years away in the Serpens constellation

sun's gravitational influence, where orbiting objects can turn around and return closer to our sun.

The sun's heliosphere doesn't extend quite as far. The heliosphere is the bubble created by the solar wind – a stream of electrically charged gas blowing outward from the sun in all directions. The boundary where the solar wind is abruptly slowed by pressure from interstellar gases is called the termination shock. This edge occurs between 80-100 astronomical units.

Two NASA spacecraft, launched in 1977, have crossed the termination shock: Voyager 1 in 2004 and Voyager 2 in 2007. But it will be many thousands of years before the two Voyagers exit the Oort Cloud.

Our solar system, the only place we know of that sustains life, formed about 4.5 billion years ago from a dense cloud of interstellar gas and dust. The cloud collapsed, possibly due to the shockwave of a nearby exploding star, called a supernova. When this dust cloud collapsed, it formed a solar nebula – a spinning, swirling disk of material.

At the centre, gravity pulled more and more material in. Eventually

A solar system is one star (ours is the sun) plus all of the objects that travel around it – planets, moons, asteroids, comets and meteoroids. Most stars are hosts to their own planets, so it is probable that there are tens of billions of other solar systems in the Milky Way galaxy alone. Solar systems can also have more than one star and are then called binary star systems if there are two stars, or multi-star systems if there are three or more stars.

'Our' solar system is located in an outer spiral arm of the vast Milky Way galaxy. It consists of the sun and everything that orbits around it. This includes the eight planets and their natural satellites (such as our moon), dwarf planets and their satellites, as well as asteroids, comets and countless particles of smaller debris.

Our solar system extends much farther than the eight planets that orbit the sun. The solar system also includes the Kuiper Belt that lies past Neptune's orbit. This is a sparsely occupied ring of icy bodies, almost all smaller than the most popular Kuiper Belt Object, the dwarf planet Pluto.

And beyond the fringes of the Kuiper belt is the Oort Cloud. This giant spherical shell surrounds our solar system. It has never been directly observed, but its existence is predicted based on mathematical models and observations of comets that probably originate from there.

The Oort Cloud is made up of icy pieces of space debris the size of mountains and sometimes larger, orbiting our sun as far as 1.6 light years away. This shell of material is thick, extending from 5,000 astronomical units to 100,000 astronomical units. One astronomical unit (or AU) is the distance from the sun to Earth, or about 93 million miles (150 million kilometres). The Oort Cloud is the boundary of the

RIGHT: Deep Space Antenna, Goldstone, California

BELOW LEFT: Voyager 2 was launched on Aug. 20, 1977 from the NASA Kennedy Space Center at Cape Canaveral in Florida where it was propelled into space on a Titan/Centaur rocket

BELOW L-R: Images taken by Voyager 2: Neptune I Uranus I Triton I Jupiter I Saturn